Praise for *Presidential Leadership*

"Only a leader of the caliber of Brent Taylor could have come up with this unique and masterfully written new book. The truths found in this volume you hold in your hands have not emerged from some lofty, esoteric ideology but have been beaten out on the anvil of Brent's own personal experience in leadership. Read every word of it and then … lead on."

O.S. Hawkins
President/CEO, GuideStone Financial Resources
Author of the *Code Series* and *VIP: Learning to Influence with Vision, Integrity, and Purpose*

"Dr. Brent Taylor has done it again! A masterful job authoring a powerful book full of great insights and inspiration. This is a must read for leaders."

Adam Wright, Ph.D.
President, Dallas Baptist University

"As a nation we are a collection of stories, representing the triumphs of high achievement and, at our worst, the loss of our humanity. For better or worse we have looked to our highest leaders for wisdom and guidance as a country during these times. In Dr. Taylor's book *Presidential Leadership* he masterfully explores the leadership lessons and warnings from those placed in the most powerful position in our nation. While our leaders are fully human and far from perfect, to quote Teddy Roosevelt, "The credit belongs to the man in the arena." This book will enlighten, teach, inspire, and encourage every person who reads it."

Tony Bridwell
Author of *Saturday Morning Tea and*
The Power of Story to Change Everything

"Dr. Brent Taylor gives us a unique and fresh perspective on twenty-one of our presidents, shining a light on their victories and pulling back the curtain on their struggles. In doing so, he teaches us powerful lessons of leadership learned in the White House and helps us apply them in our own houses. He has poured himself into this special work and I cannot more highly recommend it to every man and woman who feels called to lead—including YOU."

The Honorable Jeff Leach
Texas State Representative

"Dr. Brent Taylor's skillful storytelling offers insight into leadership qualities of our most celebrated presidents as they respond to demanding moments in our country's history. *Presidential Leadership* is a dynamic and entertaining read."

Jay C. Henry
President, North Dallas Bank Addison

"By making the past come alive, Brent Taylor causes present challenges to become significant opportunities for today's leaders. He serves as an expert yet accessible curator in *Presidential Leadership*, highlighting key principles and moments from these larger-than-life figures. He is unmatched in his ability to make these leaders from the past helpful in the present."

J. Nick Pitts, Ph.D.
Fellow, Institute for Global Engagement at Dallas Baptist University

"Dr. Brent Taylor's *Presidential Leadership* is the perfect combination of history with practical leadership lessons. For those who love American history, and especially presidential history, his book recounts some well-known—and some obscure—decisions faced by various U.S. presidents and gleans from those decisions practical advice we can apply in our own lives to become better leaders and decision makers. I am convinced that everyone will find this book to be a valuable resource in their library and an important tool for enhancing their own leadership skills."

Glen A. Blanscet
Author of *Lessons from Solomon: Finding True Success in Life*

"Every leader will draw great lessons from Dr. Brent Taylor's *Presidential Leadership*. He masterfully uses historical stories of past presidents to provide a road map and guide to all of us in the present. *Presidential Leadership* provides clarity on what's really important for you as a leader and the legacy you will leave behind."

Wally Gomaa
CEO, ACAP Healthworks

"The highest office in the United States is not only the seat of power for our nation; it is also the heartbeat of our nation's conscience. Within the president lies the ability to make a population rise to our highest potential or fall to our lowest capacity. In *Presidential Leadership: What Presidents Can Teach You About Being a Better Leader*, Dr. Brent Taylor expertly dissects the legacies of our nation's leaders to extract the wisdom we should all follow to inspire our own leadership journeys. An incredible read."

Nona Jones
International Speaker and Author, *Success from the Inside Out*

"Dr. Brent Taylor is a triple threat. His thorough knowledge of our nation's story, his well-placed humor, plus his ability to mine history for its lessons in leadership is what makes *Presidential Leadership* a must read."

Grant Skeldon
Founder of Initiative Network, and author of *The Passion Generation*

Presidential Leadership

Presidential LEADERSHIP

What Presidents Can Teach You About Being a Better Leader

DR. BRENT TAYLOR
with Mindi Bach

NEW YORK

LONDON • NASHVILLE • MELBOURNE • VANCOUVER

Presidential Leadership
What Presidents Can Teach You About Being a Better Leader

© 2021 Dr. Brent Taylor with Mindi Bach

Published in New York, New York, by Morgan James Publishing. Morgan James is a trademark of Morgan James, LLC. www.MorganJamesPublishing.com

ISBN 9781642799835 paperback
ISBN 9781642799842 eBook
Library of Congress Control Number: 2020900877

Cover & Interior Design by:
Christopher Kirk
www.GFSstudio.com

Morgan James is a proud partner of Habitat for Humanity Peninsula and Greater Williamsburg. Partners in building since 2006.

Get involved today! Visit
MorganJamesPublishing.com/giving-back

This book is dedicated to Presidential Leadership Scholars—and particularly the greatest class, 2016. Thank you for demonstrating how much can be accomplished when we, regardless of our political differences, work together to create a better world.

Table of Contents

Foreword

Our fortieth president, Ronald Reagan, looked at leadership the way Tom Sawyer painted his family's picket fence: not only by doing some of the work himself but by getting other people to do it for him. "The greatest leader," Reagan maintained, "is not necessarily the one who does the greatest things. He is the one that gets people to do the greatest things."

Brent Taylor does a little of both. Without question he has done great things. For over two decades he has successfully pastored a congregation of over 4,000 souls at First Baptist Church in Carrollton, Texas, leading a team of several ministers. He's also an adjunct professor at Dallas Baptist University, where he teaches classes on various aspects of U.S. history. And if that's not enough he's the president of Unlimited Partnerships, a mentoring organization for ministers throughout the United States and around the world.

It was his prodigious record of leadership and accomplishment that led to him be selected for the 2016 class of the Presidential Leadership Scholars. The program, initiated by Presidents George W. Bush and Bill

Clinton in 2015, serves as a catalyst for bringing together a diverse network of leaders to make a greater difference in the world by drawing on the leadership lessons from their own presidencies and those of George H.W. Bush and Lyndon Johnson.

But Dr. Taylor also wants *other* people to do great things—and to become leaders in their own right. Not later, but *now*. And at a time of division and discord, we could use good, strong leaders, those who bring us together to do, well, great things. This book will help. As Dr. Taylor writes in this introduction, it "sets out to plant new ideas in the soil of leadership growth" with the hope that they will "grow and flourish and dream new dreams."

As with the Presidential Leadership Scholars program, the soil that *he* uses to plant ideas on the subject of leadership was spread by our presidents. It turns out to be fertile ground. Who better to exemplify the best in leadership than those who practiced it at the highest level, often during the most trying of times? Dr. Taylor has taken a hard, incisive look at twenty-one of our nation's chief executives. By pairing them off, often in surprising but compelling combinations, he's able to shed light on the qualities that made them worthy of the power they held: the resolute decisiveness of George W. Bush and Harry Truman; the persuasive prowess of Lyndon Johnson and James Madison; the power to inspire imbued by Barack Obama and John Kennedy.

Optimism, as any good leader can tell you, is a virtue of its own. Abraham Lincoln, an optimist despite battling depression throughout his life, wrote of one of his predecessors, Zachary Taylor, "The presidency, even to the most experienced politicians is no bed of roses; and Gen. Taylor like others, found thorns within it." Likewise, there are thorns in the character of our presidents. All of them had their flaws and foibles. Some ultimately succeeded, others failed, most ended up somewhere in the middle. But in his examination of the presidents he covers, Dr. Taylor, also an optimist, doesn't dwell on their failings. In a cynical age, he wisely chooses to see the best in them and how those qualities brought out the best in their terms in office. Ultimately, all of them made a difference in their own way.

And so has Brent Taylor. With *Presidential Leadership*, he makes a significant contribution to presidential scholarship, but also in helping to develop new leaders who can make a difference themselves. So grab a brush and start painting—and, just as importantly, see if you can lead others to do the same.

Mark K. Updegrove

Mark K. Updegrove is the president and CEO of the LBJ Foundation, and the former director of the LBJ Presidential Library. The author of four books on the presidency including *The Last Republicans: Inside the Extraordinary Relationship Between George H.W. Bush and George W. Bush* and *Indomitable Will: LBJ in the Presidency,* Updegrove is the presidential historian for ABC News and has conducted exclusive interviews with five U.S. presidents. He and his wife Amy live in Austin, Texas

Introduction

I have scheduled a leadership meeting every Saturday morning. Before you think I'm a terrible boss for dragging my team into morning meetings on a weekend, let me assure you that I'm not that cruel. Instead, I have a standing Saturday morning appointment with my teenage son. Like me, he is an early riser, so we hit a local breakfast spot right when the doors open. Over coffee, eggs, and pancakes, we talk about life and spend precious time together. This is my favorite meeting of the week. We even call it "Leadership Meeting," and it turns out he's a great teacher.

I strongly desire that my three children are great leaders. I do not mean that they *become* great leaders in the future when my two oldest are out of college and my youngest son leaves home. I mean that I want them to be great leaders right *now*. Leadership is not a position we attain. It's a mindset we live. In my career, I have observed leaders in boardrooms and classrooms, sports fields and the political arena, the military and the church. Some of the greatest leaders I have ever encountered are completely unknown to the masses. Leadership is not a function of popularity. At the highest office in the United States, however, there are a few leaders familiar to everyone who have each left their mark on history.

Twenty-one of these leaders are profiled in this book. Yet, the book is not primarily about them. This book is about leadership and how decisions and actions made in the White House can apply to what takes place in offices, locker rooms, classrooms, and across the table at breakfast. This book highlights the leadership actions modeled by the presidents and how they are applicable in your life and mine.

I also want to tell you what this book is not. In what I believe to be some of the greatest political writing in our nation's history, Abraham Lincoln (after whom I named my son), wrote these powerful words:

> *With malice toward none, with charity for all, with firmness in the right as God gives us to see the right, let us strive on to finish the work we are in, to bind up the nation's wounds, to care for him who shall have borne the battle and for his widow and his orphan, to do all which may achieve and cherish a just and lasting peace among ourselves and with all nations.*

Those words wonderfully illustrate the tone in which this book is intentionally written—*with malice toward none and charity to all.*

This book is not meant to be a complete history of each administration, nor is it a treatise on the morality of each man. All of our leaders have faults, and I have not sought to point out each one of them. Rather, I have sought to be honest about faults and failings, but have not tried to list all of them. This book sets out to plant new ideas in the soil of leadership growth, not join the volumes intent on digging up dirt.

Will some prefer that I had made a disparaging remark about one or more of the leaders with whom they hold political differences? Probably. Our culture has morphed into an "us vs. them" environment that affects the way we read (and read into) everything. I want to invite you to try to set any tribalism aside and read toward the spirit of the book. That is, to learn lessons on how to be a better leader in your sphere of influence to make the world a better place.

On Twitter, people often say, "Retweets ≠ endorsements." Just because I have pointed out a leadership trait or policy decision doesn't equate to my endorsement. We simply must be able to look and learn without assuming every word is an endorsement of policy or position. Also, as a historian, I am aware it will take a great deal of time before the legacies of some of these men and the effectiveness of some of their legislative decisions will be fully understood. In other words, when it comes to comments about policies, think of it like perfume—sniff it but don't drink it.

I strongly desire that you are a great leader right *now*. Consider this book your Saturday Leadership Meeting—intent to inspire you to grow and flourish and to dream new dreams. No matter your age or circumstance, you play an important leadership role. Spending breakfast with men who have held one of the most intense, stressful jobs in history is an invitation to draw from a deep well of resources. And as you apply what you learn, may you embody what Abraham Lincoln called us to do in his first inaugural address. May we all appeal to the "better angels of our nature" as we lead others into a bright future.

Now back to breakfast.

Brent Taylor

Chapter 1

George Washington

Incarnational Leadership—

The Gold Standard of Presidential Leadership

*"I walk on untrodden ground. There is scarcely any part of my
conduct which may not hereafter be drawn into precedent."*
–George Washington

"I love a parade."
–Harry Richmond

"I am honored with the commands of the Senate to wait upon your Excellency with the information of your being elected to the office of President of the United States of America." On

April 14, 1789, in the quiet of his Mount Vernon home, George Washington received the news that would launch his journey to New York to assume the office of the first president of the United States—the only president ever elected by unanimous vote.

His visitor, Secretary of Congress Charles Thomson, was a trusted friend, patriot, and partner in shaping the republic. Thomson continued, reading a letter from Senator John Langdon, "Suffer me, sir, to indulge the hope that so auspicious a mark of public confidence will meet your approbation and be considered as a sure pledge of the affection and support you are to expect from a free and enlightened people."[1]

Washington was officially called back into public service—to the highest position in the land. A position yet untested and unestablished, Washington's leadership would be crucial for the survival of the nation and the future of the government. His wife of thirty years looked on, acknowledging that their quiet respite in Mount Vernon would forever be changed. After careful thought, Washington remarked, "While I realize the arduous nature of the task which is conferred on me and feel my inability to perform it, I wish there may not be reason for regretting the choice. All I can promise is only that which can be accomplished by an honest zeal." With this humble acknowledgment, the man who had only completed a primary education, who led the Revolution, and helped shape the Constitution, embarked on a journey-turned-parade-route to his new post.

Crowned with laurel, he rode past crowds of townspeople, musicians, flower-laden maidens and fleets of ships. He gave speeches, was received at dinners, and was called the "savior of the country" to the peal of church bells. Fatigued from his 18th-century ticker-tape parade, he attempted to quietly slip into New York at the end of his journey to no avail. The country had waited for a leader to embody everything left unwritten in the Constitution, and everyone turned out to celebrate. There was one man who emerged as the true leader of the fledgling nation, and just like the savior to whom he was compared, the government rested on his shoulders.

As we embark upon this leadership journey through the presidential administrations from the founding of the United States to present day, George Washington stands tallest. With no one to go before him, his courageous actions have shaped the forty-four to succeed him in office. Examining his leadership will shape our understanding of all the others.

The proverbial question of leadership is, "Are leaders born or are they made?" While the consensus among students of leadership would most often tell you they are made, on February 22, 1732, a true leader was born. Though not considered overtly winsome, George Washington would be a leader among leaders and would endear himself not only to his men but draw a nation into his cult of personality. His story is not one of rags to riches, but in a society that did not emphasize the study of leadership skills, Washington seemed to be innately born with the ability to lead men. This first child of Augustine and Mary Ball Washington would become first among equals long before he became first at war, first at peace, and first in the heart of his countrymen.

Very little is known of Washington's early life except that his parents raised him with a strong work ethic and sense of character. Though the story of the cherry tree is certainly apocryphal, George was reared to be honest, straightforward, and strong. Young George never attended college, and after the death of his father, his formal education probably ended around the age of fifteen.

Washington's early occupation as a surveyor would ultimately lead him into the army. Washington loved the soldier's life and it would become a very important part of who he was as a leader. After fighting the crown and leading the colonies in their eight-year war for independence, the subsequent victory at Yorktown meant it was nation-building time. Washington was thrust into a place of great influence and leadership at the Second Continental Congress.

When called upon to serve, Washington again heeded the call of the nation to become the first President of the United States. He not only established what presidents did, but more importantly, who they *were*. He was not only the first president, he *was* the presidency itself. He did what leaders are supposed to do—lead. But more than that, Washington *was* the cause; he *was* the military; he *was* the leader; and he *was* the nation. George Washington was our nation's most important *Incarnational Leader*.

INCARNATIONAL LEADERSHIP: LEADERS EMBODY THEIR ORGANIZATION

This book will focus on what leaders *do*—based on the actions presidents have taken in and out of office. However, leadership is first and foremost about *being*. Until a leader understands who they are and what they represent, they will never be able to address properly how they must act. Can an individual lead without understanding the idea of being? Of course. But, the leader who understands who they are, and combines that with a clear knowledge of what they need to do, will command more influence.

There is a fundamental difference between being and doing. Leaders who only focus on doing miss out on the best part of leadership—seeing others rise because they believe in what the leader represents. Great leaders embody a principle known as Incarnational Leadership. Incarnational Leadership is not about messaging or strategy or ROI, but is the leader, him or herself, embodying the organization's cause and vision.

The word "incarnational" literally means "in the flesh" and these leaders are the organization in human form. Living in Texas, I frequently eat my favorite dish of cheese enchiladas. If you have never been to Texas and had a cheese enchilada, I have officially added an item to your bucket list. These particular enchiladas are filled with cheese and onions and then are smothered with *chili con carne*—chili with meat. The word *carne* means "meat" or "flesh." The word *carne* is also present in other portions of our vocabulary. Great leaders are *incarnational*, literally representing their organization "in the flesh."

According to the Oxford English Dictionary, the word incarnational means *to be an expression of or give tangible or visible presence to an idea, quality, or feeling*. Incarnational leaders become a physical representation of the goals and dreams of an organization. They visibly embody what the organization believes in, represents, and aspires to become. To understand the essence of the organization, one should not have to look any further than the leader.

While there are many great examples of leaders who embody the organization (Steve Jobs of Apple, Jack Welch of General Electric, Walt Disney of The Walt Disney Company, or Mark Zuckerberg of Facebook, Inc), there are very few people in history to become more emblematic of a cause or position than George Washington. From his allies John Adams, Thomas Jefferson, and French officer the Marquis de Lafayette—to his enemies such as King George III—all people knew George Washington represented the American Revolution. Benjamin Franklin warned the Continental Congress that they all must hang together or surely they would all hang separately. No Founding Father would have swung higher or longer than George Washington had the Revolution gone the way most of the world believed it would.

George Washington *was* the Revolution. Enemies and allies alike knew he was the Revolution. And no one was more keenly aware than George Washington himself. From the first meetings of the Second Continental Congress, Washington appeared in his military uniform. If ever there was someone who followed the maxim "dress for the job you want," Washington was that man. He looked the part of commander in chief years before he was officially in the position.

THERE ARE NO ORANGES INSIDE BANANAS: INCARNATIONAL LEADERS HAVE INTEGRITY

One of the strange realities of our world is that the older our planet becomes, the more we tend to move away from reality. Artificial intelligence, virtual reality, and "fake news" have become mainstays of our conversations, yet there is a yearning within people to have deeper relationships and an experience with authenticity. While there are many books, articles, and podcasts on leadership, what followers need are Incarnational Leaders who often reflect the persona of a good parent—a role of leadership that embodies a very clear sense of values and character.

Once the new nation was established and Washington was elected, the new leader of the fledgling nation recognized that the decisions he was making would outlive him. For this reason, Washington remained acutely aware of his actions and choices. Some of those precedents established by the first president include a two-term presidency, the words "So help me God" at the end of the oath of office, the establishment of a cabinet and the tradition of delivering a farewell address. As Washington was establishing the role and practices of the presidency, he was at the same time becoming the parent of the country—a father with a clear sense of values and character.

Values and character are not a couple of "think positive" buzzwords but are critical components to Incarnational Leadership. Good leaders know what they believe, why they believe it, and how to put those beliefs into practice. Followers struggle with unmarked trails while Incarnational Leaders illuminate the pathway with the expression of the values they hold dear. When the pathway seems unclear or ever confusing, the followers trust the character of the leader.

One universal leadership value found at the core of good character is integrity. Integrity makes good leaders effective. When this piece is missing from the puzzle, the whole picture is not only incomplete, but blurred. As I often say, God makes things with integrity. You will never peel a banana and find an orange. Leaders with integrity are trustworthy and enjoy the respect, admiration, and loyalty of those who follow them.

As I wrote in my previous book, *Founding Leadership*, George Washington understood the importance of values in his life and leadership. As a young man, he wrote down by hand and committed to maintaining a set of principles and guidelines called *The Rules of Civility and Decent Behavior*. These maxims stated such altruistic ideas as, "Turn not your back to others especially in speaking," or "Show not yourself glad at the misfortune of another though he were your enemy." Washington didn't just write those down, he put them into practice for the benefit of his own life and the lives of generations in the nation he was building.

BASIC PRINCIPLES: INCARNATIONAL LEADERS ARE GUIDED BY A PERSONAL CONSTITUTION

Nobody wants to receive a "Dear John" letter. However, at the dawn of the republic, this was exactly what was needed. The Declaration of Independence was the greatest break-up letter of all time. It opened the door for a document that established new, healthy relationships. The United States Constitution is a living, breathing birth certificate and marriage covenant all rolled into one. It embodies the values we hold as a nation and guides the decision-making of our country. While only 4,543 words written over 116 days, the document has endured tempest and trial. From day one, the Founding Fathers knew it would need repairs (amendments) and maintenance, but what was written in Independence Hall between May 25, 1787, and September 17, 1787, would survive and thrive through today.

One of the reasons why the Constitution has stood the test of time is because it was written to form guardrails around the cliffs that threaten the fall of democracy. The Founding Fathers understood the necessity of interpretation and revision, but they also knew that the fundamental principles contained within would last for the life of the republic. Those guardrails are in place for a reason and their permanent nature helps to define who we are.

In the same way, Incarnational Leaders must be guided by a personal, written "constitution." As a college professor, I often work with young millennials on developing a document for their lives that will provide a tangible reminder of who they are and what they aspire to be. Like the U.S. Constitution, this document is not to be changed with every career move or milestone, but is a representation of the values and beliefs that they will embody for a lifetime.

For any leader, the exercise of recording a personal constitution is an experience that helps define values, goals, talents, and mission. This personal constitution is not the cosmetics of makeup and hair—it's blood and guts, sweat, and sometimes tears. It represents who you are on the inside. Just like we have amended our founding document, so there may be amendments to your personal constitution. But the core doesn't change. It defines you and, in essence, embodies you. Your personal constitution expresses who you are, helps you know yourself, and allows others to understand who you are. I challenge every leader who wants to be incarnational to develop their own personal constitution—their own guiding, defining document.

ROLL CALL—INCARNATIONAL LEADERS HAVE A UNIQUE ROLE IN THE ORGANIZATION

Steve Jobs once said, "Management is about persuading people to do things they do not want to do, while leadership is about inspiring people to do things they never thought they could." Many times, leaders forget the distinct differences played by different roles in an organization.

I generally categorize people into four categories. There are leaders, bosses, managers, and followers. One of the biggest misconceptions of these categories is that managers are always leaders. In fact, managers almost always assume they are leaders but rarely are. Managers are a very important part of an organization because they help accomplish the vision by taking care of the details. They are more often focused on the process, a set plan, and resolving issues or problems quickly and efficiently. Managers tend to say no if the budget must be squeezed too much or the risk is too high. They believe in people but their focus is policy and procedures. All organizations need managers, but the best organizations look for people who are leaders first and have the ability to also manage.

In the same way, it is difficult to distinguish at times between leaders and bosses. Both are in charge, both often have the loudest voices in the room, and both names are often used synonymously. For example, the question might be asked, "Who is the leader of your organization?" and the answer is given, "Susan." That same question might be posed, "Who's the boss around here?" Our culture uses the terms interchangeably but the dynamic is far from the same. Theodore Roosevelt once said, "People ask the difference between a leader and a boss. The leader leads and the boss drives."

Leaders are neither bosses nor managers. They have the best attributes of both, but attain a level of responsibility the manager or boss will rarely experience. Leaders—while wholly set apart—view themselves as fellow team members who are helping the entire group accomplish the goal. Their vocabulary is marked by the word "We" as opposed to the boss who struggles with the proverbial "I" problem. Leaders don't just tell people where the trenches are; they are also out front leading the troops. While bosses often prey on fear among the followers, leaders thrive on enthusiasm. Ultimately, as E.M. Kelley said,

> *"The difference between a boss and a leader: a boss says, 'Go! —* *a leader says, 'Let's go!'"*

From his first battle to his parade towards the presidency, Washington knew how to balance his command-and-control leadership while also influencing all roles in his respective organizations. Leadership is influence, and Washington operated in this realm, understanding it is the most powerful method of motivating people. Although there were times he had to take clear control of a situation and "boss" his men into action, he recognized this as just a tool in his leader's toolbox. Incarnational Leaders know their role and inspire followers with "Let's go."

Think about your own style of leadership. Are you a manager, a boss, or a leader? How does your personal constitution help you define your role? Once defined, your role can—and should—be shared with the next generation.

WALK WITH ME—LEADERS PREPARE THE NEXT GENERATION

We live in a unique time in American history. Never have we had a larger population in the country and more importantly, so many generations alive at the same time. Today's generations are unique and well defined. From the Greatest Generation to the millennial and the new Generation Z, it is clear the multitude of generations not only makes our nation bigger, but stronger.

Millennials have become a force in today's culture, upending the norms of business, redefining success, and frustrating countless older supervisors in all areas of industry. But the fact that millennials are different from previous generations only makes sense. Think about what millennials have never experienced. Millennials weren't alive when MTV only played music videos, have never forgotten to rewind a VCR tape, don't have a clue what a floppy disk is, and have never had film developed. They don't know what it's like to miss a television show and not be able to ever see it again (except maybe, just maybe, in the summer). And while they can type on their phones with both thumbs, they are clueless when it comes to a rotary dial telephone. Millennials know about remote controls on televisions, but fail to realize that when I was a kid, *I was* the remote control.

Millennials have ushered in a lot change as they have entered the workforce. Unlike previous generations, millennials want a place at the table today. They want to express their opinions and do not think they have to wait until they reach their mid-40s to contribute. They are less interested in power suits, power lunches, and corner offices than they are a job that brings significance, allows for facial hair, and offers a really good cup of coffee. Ultimately, they want freedom to be themselves and be able to leave their work at the office when they go home.

There is something else millennials desperately pursue—millennials are yearning for mentoring. In recent years, there has been an increase in the use of the term "mentoring." There are many reasons this term has taken off, but one of the primary reasons is the rise of the millennial. This generation, more than most others, longs to have someone invest in their lives and show them the way.

This desire for mentors by millennials is one of the greatest opportunities for Incarnational Leaders. Mentoring is not just telling people what to do. It's not Dear Abby over coffee. Mentoring is not even about pointing to a good role model. Mentoring is about an invitation—the invitation to come and walk with me. It's about a relationship designed to share life with another person. Whereas coaching is designed to improve current performance, mentoring is a long-term sharing of life experience. Because Incarnational Leadership is not simply about business models, product development, and ROI, mentoring is the perfect opportunity to demonstrate what it means to embody the values of a leader and the organization.

Washington was consistently mentoring someone. His most famous pupil was Alexander Hamilton. Hamilton needed Washington, but like most mentors discover, Washington also needed Hamilton. Both men were made better by their mentoring relationship. Hamilton was able to see the "Glorious Cause" lived out in his daily interaction with the General. Hamilton believed in the cause before he enlisted, but there is little doubt that his passion increased exponentially as he walked with Washington. Washington embodied the Revolution and Hamilton was inspired by the same vision too.

Make a conscious effort to evaluate who in your organization can benefit from a mentoring relationship. Then, invite them to take a walk by your side. You may just find that you need them—beards, coffee, and all—just as much as they need you. If you are a millennial leader, it is never too early to mentor a peer.

Join the Parade

On April 16, 1789, two days after Charles Thompson delivered the news to the newly elected president, George Washington left Mount Vernon and set out by carriage to assume his new post. Once called, he did not hesitate to act quickly upon his duty.

As I began this chapter, I said leadership is inherently about being— that Incarnational Leaders embody the organization. It is who they are and, in many ways, it is who the organization becomes. A leader who embodies their business communicates the values of the organization and sets the direction just by the sheer power of who they are. George Washington was a force of nature simply by the man he was. As he sat in the seat of power, Washington became the face of the Revolution and, ultimately, the Presidency.

But leaders can't simply sit around and be. Leadership is about doing and Washington did not sit around and simply *think* about who he was. Washington was a man of action and he operated from a position of getting the job done.

Incarnational Leadership is both embodying the vision (incarnational) and acting upon that vision (leadership).

And that's what the rest of this book is about. This is a book primarily about doing. With George Washington as the foundation, the other twenty presidents paired in these chapters will put the action into Incarnational Leadership.

Just like George Washington, there is something you are called to do in leadership—a life purpose standing at your threshold. Before you receive that knock on the door, first understand who you are and what you embody. Then, when your life and your mission line up, come walk with me as we knock on the door of our nation's leaders and become strengthened by how they acted upon their calling.

Get ready to join the parade and walk on previously untrodden ground. All I can promise is only that which can be accomplished by an honest zeal. You were born for this. Let's go!

Chapter 2

Bill Clinton & James K. Polk

Leaders Follow Their North Star

"We need to think like Ferrari."
−Ford v. Ferrari

*"For all that has been said, I don't know what I'm going to say
because we've had several messages—one from the president,
which could be a sermon from a pulpit anywhere."*
−Reverend Billy Graham, Oklahoma City, April 23, 1995

O n April 19, 1995, four toddlers were dozing in their cribs in
the America's Kids Daycare Center in the Alfred P. Murrah
Federal building in Oklahoma City. Twenty-one children, five
years of age and younger, were fed breakfast by three teachers, who would

15

also lead them in their morning music. The children's parents—a mix of double income households and single parents—were already at their desks, grateful for the program that allowed the opportunity for lunchtime visits.

At 9:00 a.m., a Ryder rental truck full of ammonium nitrate fertilizer and diesel fuel parked in front of the daycare windows, just feet from the children. Two minutes later, 4,800 pounds of explosives detonated, obliterating one third of the federal building and killing 168 people. In the daycare, only two children survived. It was as if the planet stopped moving as Americans stared in horror at the now Pulitzer Prize—winning image of firefighter Chris Fields cradling the lifeless, bloodied body of one-year-old Baylee Almon.

The country was in need of a leader to make sense of the loss, offer a response, and give confidence that the future had hope.

When President Bill Clinton stepped up to the podium at the memorial service, his pensive and compassionate demeanor set the stage for one of his most masterful moments. The arena was filled with a multigenerational mix of dignitaries and everyday citizens, all reeling from the worst terrorist attack to have ever occurred on American soil. With the passion of a minister, the empathy of a father, the justice of an avenger, and the healing hands of a physician, he eloquently addressed the anger, fear, despair, and helplessness that had hung in the air the preceding week—while acknowledging the unprecedented sacrifice and support of Oklahoma City and the American people. He firmly stated his administration's commitment to rebuild the city, heal the injured, and bring the perpetrators to justice. He quoted scripture about the personal responsibility to avoid hatred, talked of the dogwood tree he planted at the White House as a sign of hope and opportunity, and praised the community for holding each other up.

This was—and is—Bill Clinton: a leader guided by his personal, deep-held philosophy that humanity at its best unites around similarities and embraces responsibility, opportunity, and community. A leader with eyes on the present and a mind fully focused on the future where both personal and communal destiny become something greater.

In 1845, James K. Polk also stepped into the presidency with his eyes on the republic and his mind on its future. His guiding star pointed back to earth as Manifest Destiny—a belief in expanding the landmass of the republic as an expression of American exceptionalism, virtue, and irresistible duty. He was not an orator or storyteller like Bill Clinton, but his dogged personal belief in the future destiny of the nation developed the passion needed in his leadership. As a result of his convictions, the eleventh president was able to, in only one term, annex Texas and ultimately the entire southwest, as well as the present-day states of Washington, Oregon, and Idaho, with parts of Montana and Wyoming. In fact, Polk added more territory to the United States in one term than any other president in history. Eschewing critics, Polk set his course and accomplished exactly what he set out to do.

Had the eleventh president and the forty-second met for a stargazing session, they may have noted that Polk favored Orion the Hunter with his nonthreatening stance and subtle armor available for a push westward. And they may have agreed that Clinton favored Taurus the Bull—the poised, strong, watchful, tenacious guardian of the celestial community. But both would have cast their vision on the North Star—the guiding light and fixed point around which everything else gravitates. With very strong spouses to prod them forward, both presidents held an unwavering gaze on their true north—the principles and philosophies that permeated all of their policies and lit their way amidst constellations of critics.

The presidencies of Bill Clinton and James Polk—with all of their bright stars and explosive supernovas, are testaments to leaders who follow a guiding star that enlightens and charts their life story.

FORD V. FERRARI—LEADERS DEVELOP A PERSONAL, PHILOSOPHICAL CONTRACT

Many humbling moments of my parenting have occurred at the bowling alley with my young children. Thanks to new technology, bumpers would automatically raise for my children as they stumbled toward the lane with their bowling ball. While they heaved their ball into the lane, we would all patiently watch it slowly bump and bounce its way to a guaranteed connection with the pins. This, in turn, guaranteed parental applause. But for me, there were no bumpers, and I quickly realized my *Kingpin* days were far behind me. On more occasions than I like to admit, my ball veered into the gutter, rolling right past the pins and out of sight. My kids would giggle as the machine reset the ten pins, which were still standing undisturbed.

In the same way, leaders are often caught watching their efforts roll right past the people they hoped to affect, because they have never developed the personal framework to keep them in their lane. This was the lesson Ford Motor Company learned when it faced Ferrari at Le Mans in 1966. In the movie depicting this historic battle for world domination between car manufacturers, Lee Iacocca, vice president of Ford Motor Company, said "Enzo Ferrari will go down in history as the greatest car manufacturer of all time. Why? Is it because he built the most cars? No. It's because of what his cars mean. Victory. Ferrari wins at Le Mans. People, they want some of that victory. What if the Ford badge meant victory?"[2]

Iacocca knew that Ferrari embodied its vision and philosophy. It wasn't just a business; it was a brand that reflected the personal philosophy of its owner. This philosophy moved the automotive community to embrace and revere its greatness and vision. Iacocca knew that Ford had to stop and reflect on what defined it and recommit to its guiding vision.

Don't Stop Thinkin' About Tomorrow

President Clinton was a Ferrari in the White House: smooth-talking, operating with impressive speed, carving the corners, and guided by his personal contract to see the finish line while connecting with the people in his lane. Raised by grandparents in humble surroundings, young "Billy" regularly attended the Baptist church, enjoying its soulful music and message. According to Stephanie Streett, executive director of the Clinton Foundation, "You can't talk about Bill Clinton without talking about his faith." This is what shaped his personal philosophical contract, which he articulated to the nation by leveraging the biblical phrase "New Covenant" to describe his vision. His New Covenant consisted of three parts: responsibility, community, and opportunity. In his acceptance speech at the Democratic Convention in 1992, he passionately outlined this New Covenant for America:

> *I call this approach a New Covenant, a solemn agreement between the people and their government, based not simply on what each of us can take, but what all of us must give our nation ... What is the vision of our New Covenant? An America with millions of new jobs in dozens of new industries moving confidently into the twenty-first century. An America that says to entrepreneurs and business people: we will give you more incentives and opportunity than ever before ... but you must do your part. You must be responsible ... The New Covenant is also about more than opportunities and responsibilities for you and your families. It is also about your common community ... In the end, my fellow Americans, this New Covenant simply asks us all to be Americans again. Old-fashioned Americans for a new time.*[3]

Stephanie Streett, who has known the president since her youth, noted that there is not one piece of legislation that outshines the other in illustrating the president's New Covenant. His philosophy permeated everything he did—from education choice to welfare reform, technology,

NAFTA, even health care reform—he saw these efforts as more of a philosophy than legislation to be implemented. He was always focused on the endgame—constantly analyzing how each policy would affect each segment of society and how that would play into the future. "Are people better off when I stopped than when I started?" was the question that mattered most to Clinton.

Nobody understood that better than a young White House employee named Silvia Matthews. Matthews was a junior staffer from a small town who had the privilege of serving in Clinton's administration. During a policy meeting, the president stopped, turned to Sylvia, who was seated at the back of the room, and asked her opinion of how she thought this would affect the citizens of her small town. The president didn't just care about people, he noticed them, listened to their opinions, and made sure they were not forgotten in the greater story.

In his book *Where Have All the Leaders Gone?* Lee Iacocca poses several questions to Americans to think about for the future—foundational questions to ponder before rushing to judgment. In the same way, leaders must take time to understand who they are, who they want to be, and how they want to treat others, in order to fully commit to a personal philosophical contract. For Iacocca, it was the 10 Cs of leadership: (curiosity, communication, creativity, character, courage, conviction, charisma, competency, common sense, and crisis) that were born out of his reflections. Whether it's Clinton's three elements of his New Covenant, or Iacocca's 10 Cs of leadership, we must be willing to reflect and ponder the bumpers in our own personal contract that keep us squarely focused in our lane.

Leaders Write Down Goals in Their Personal Contract

Where Clinton was the sleek Ferrari of the White House, James Polk could be the American Ford—reliable, dependable, not too flashy. His personality was once described as a "wet dishrag" and John Quincy

Adams said, "He has no wit, no literature, no point of argument, no gracefulness of delivery, no eloquence of language, no philosophy, no pathos." Yet Polk was built of nuts and bolts. He was steady and driven and knew exactly what he wanted to accomplish based upon his personal belief in Manifest Destiny. When Polk took office in 1845, in a private conversation with his new navy secretary, George Bancroft, he clearly articulated his four goals and promised that if those were achieved he would not run again:

- Reestablish an independent treasury system
- Reduce tariffs
- Acquire the Oregon Territory
- Acquire California and New Mexico

Two domestic goals were combined with two very ambitious foreign policy goals. Remarkably, Polk was able to do exactly what he had promised. And true to his word, President Polk did not seek a second term, successfully meeting all four goals in just one term in office.

In the words of Lee Iacocca, "The discipline of writing something down is the first step toward making it happen." Once a personal contract is developed, writing down specific goals must follow. Venture capitalist John Doerr has developed a system for recording and following personal goals. The system is called OKR, standing for "Objectives and Key Results." His strategy has helped Intuit, Amazon, Google, Twitter and the Bill Gates Foundation to name a few. In his book *Measure What Matters*, he articulates that leaders must have *personal* OKRs to achieve goals. These personal objectives and key results are the true power of the system as they shape everything else.

Carol Shelby, the automotive designer played by Matt Damon in Ford v. Ferrari, said, "It is a truly lucky man who knows what he wants to do in this world, because that man will never work a day in his life." Both presidents Clinton and James Polk knew what they stood for, and it directed what they wanted to do and how they wanted to do it. In the words of Mark Victor Hansen, author of *Chicken Soup for the Soul*,

---

"By recording your dreams and goals on paper, you set in motion the process of becoming the person you most want to be. Put your future in good hands—your own."

LEADERS CHART A COURSE

It has been said that if you don't know where you are going, any road will get you there. Both James Polk and Bill Clinton were dark horses on the road to the Oval Office, but both knew the road they were traveling and just how to get where they were going. Having both served as governors, lawyers, and small-town citizens, they set a steady course and never wavered. Polk had overcome a battered President Martin Van Buren in the primaries, whose opposition to the annexation of Texas—the hot-button issue of the election—sealed his defeat. He then capitalized on Henry Clay's indecision on Texas and won the general election in 1844. Clinton—playing off of the economic recession in 1992, a lackluster message from President George H.W. Bush, and the American trepidation about the future—eloquently spoke into the national dread with his campaign theme song, Fleetwood Mac's "Don't Stop (Thinking about Tomorrow.)" His campaign manager coined the simple phrase, "The economy, stupid"—a call to focus the nation on the economic recovery—to entice both staff and electorate to remain on course. Once in office, both presidents set about implementing their plans.

In one of his greatest accomplishments, President Clinton developed and implemented a new nationwide service program sponsored by the federal government—a longtime goal that perfectly aligned with his New Covenant philosophy. In this program, the *responsibility* was given to America's new generation, the *opportunity* was open to all, and the *community* became known as AmeriCorps.

Keeping Your Eyes on the Apex Point

In 1963, high school student Bill Clinton was selected as a delegate to Boys Nation—a convention sponsored by the American Legion in Washington D.C. It was there that a seventeen-year-old Clinton shook the hand of President John F. Kennedy, his political idol. As president, Bill Clinton was determined to inspire a new generation of Americans the way Kennedy had inspired him and shaped his thinking. "Just think of it," he [Clinton] told the nation. "Think of it. Millions of energetic young men and women serving their country by policing the streets or teaching the children or caring for the sick. Or working with the elderly and people with disabilities. Or helping young people to stay off drugs and out of gangs, giving us all a sense of new hope and limitless possibilities."[4]

President Clinton had pondered and reflected on a program like this for years. Through careful consideration, the fabric of his personal philosophy (responsibility, community, opportunity) became the garment of his personal contract. Then he charted a course to make it happen. Under his leadership, the Community Service Trust Act was signed into law and AmeriCorps was created. In connecting the past with the future, Clinton also incorporated Kennedy's VISTA (Volunteers in Service to America) into the program. AmeriCorps remains a service program funded by the federal government and other organizations, in order to give citizens an opportunity to serve the community while learning valuable leadership skills. To date, over a million Americans have participated in the program, realizing the president's vision of serving the community in countless ways. AmeriCorps is a testament of Bill Clinton's ability to stay on course and get it done.

Bill Ford Jr.—the great-grandson of founder Henry Ford and chairman of Ford Motor Company—is an executive who also sees the endgame and has charted new territory for the company. He was first at Ford to champion sustainability and realize the value of remaining on the cutting edge of new technology in the automotive industry. He has set a course for the future of the company and the community to which Ford owes its popularity. When asked how he balances corporate and community responsibilities, Ford answered, "As leaders, we have, hopefully, some brainpower, we have connections, we have resources. And we should bring those to bear to make our communities better places—whether that's schools or hospitals or helping with social issues like homelessness and hunger. Find the thing that resonates most—but whatever it is, do it and set the example."[5]

Like President Clinton, Ford's leadership course permeated his corporate goals and his community goals. He operated with the same unwavering determination echoed in both the presidential races of Polk and Clinton: "whatever it is, do it and set the example."

Any race car driver knows that the fundamental of racing is managing the racing line—the fastest line around a corner on the racetrack. There are several points on a racing line but the key is to keep your eyes on the apex point of the curve and manage your speed. In the same way, leaders must chart a course and then cast their vision on the points that will keep them on that course. There will always be interruptions that threaten to derail plans and goals. Managing the speed and strategy around those "corners" is key to any operation. When asked how he viewed the "disruptions" of companies such as Tesla and Google, Ford commented that even "the disruptors are being disrupted themselves on a regular basis." Therefore, "there's an interesting balance that has to take place, because we need to be open to and excited by the disruption happening everywhere. But we can't be distracted by it, because we have a daily business to run."[6]

When leaders manage their "racing line," they are able to stay on course without letting the distractions of competitors and challengers into their lane. And that is where the endgame is realized and programs like AmeriCorps are able to cross the finish line.

Trust Your Gut

Even when "managing the racing line," there are often periods of time when the course is cloudy and the pathway is obscured by inside and outside influences. In those cases, it is important to "trust your gut" and hold fast to the original vision.

On the road to completing his four stated goals, President Polk faced endless challenges. Yet it was his ability to hang onto his belief in Manifest Destiny that continued to move Polk forward in some difficult times. While he often missed the apex moments of his goals, his view of the race to broaden the country from "sea to shining sea" cut through the fog of disruption. With his eyes on the endgame, Polk turned his attention to Mexico—who had been negotiating with the British about a California purchase. The Brits had also offered their support of an independent Texas, which Polk had annexed in 1845. Polk sent an envoy to Mexico to enter the negotiations and make a play for California. This triggered a Mexican revolt against its president. Polk had hoped to avoid a war with Mexico over Texas but was not afraid of fighting to get what he wanted. Eventually, conflict erupted on the border as Polk was prepared to force a showdown with the Mexican government over the Texas border.

In 1846, the Mexican army crossed the Rio Grande, leaving sixteen American soldiers dead or wounded. President Polk received a declaration of war from a very patriotic Congress. To push back the Mexican advance, and to continue with his expansionist vision, he charted a course for war and set his sights on his goal via this new path. By 1848, the war was over and the president signed the Treaty of Guadalupe Hidalgo. This "Mexican Cessation" gave one-third of its territory to the United States, which today includes Arizona, Utah, Nevada, California, much of New Mexico, and parts of Wyoming and Colorado. While criticized as an outright "land grab" and a change to the original course President Polk envisioned, he trusted his "gut" and pushed forward around the curve of the war with Mexico, in order to remain on his greater course of expansionism.

There have been many times in my career where the path forward has been obscured by uncertainty and interruption. It is in those moments I have learned to "trust my gut" in decision-making. For leaders, that "gut" should be driven by the "North Star" articulated in our personal philosophical contract. In those moments when the path is unclear, some practical questions to ask before making a decision are:

1. Does this align with my core values?
2. What am I giving up in order to move forward?
3. How will this decision affect those around me now and in the future?
4. Am I prepared for the consequences that might come from this decision?

Answer those questions, then make a decision. Adjust your speed, work the brakes if needed, and manage the new curves on the course.

STORY-WEAVING—PUTTING YOUR PERSONAL PHILOSOPHY INTO ACTION

On a recent visit to Europe, I was able to spend some time in the Vatican Museums. In the very heart of the Vatican is its Gallery of Tapestries, featuring floor-to-ceiling depictions of various religious themes. Woven in both silk and wool, some tapestries are so intricate they include the "moving perspective" where the eyes of the characters "follow you" as you walk. If you viewed the back of the tapestry, one would encounter a tangle of threads, crisscrossed and knotted in an indistinguishable pattern. The front side, however, is a true masterpiece.

This is a perfect illustration of what emerges when leaders have charted a course and put their personal philosophies into action. There are decisions and days that don't seem to fit the pattern, but ultimately, the story which is weaved throughout a lifetime can become a remarkable picture of harmony and clarity.

Develop a Plot—Leaders Value Characters in Their Story

A tapestry always tells a story. In any good story, one needs a plot and the characters to pull off the scenes. Part of preparing characters for action is development. For leaders, this investment in others is essential to building a team. So often, leaders are shaped by their own backgrounds and it colors the way they relate to the unique characters who are under their leadership.

President Clinton was indelibly shaped by the people in his early life, which in turn affected how he related to others. A master storyteller, Clinton's life is truly a fine tapestry that combines small-town perspectives with international vision. According to Bruce Lindsey, former deputy counsel to President Clinton during his eight years in office, Clinton was exceptionally close with his grandfather and that relationship shaped his ability to relate to people of all cultures and generations. President Clinton's father died before he was born and his grandparents had a primary role in raising him in the small town of Hope, Arkansas. His grandfather ran a small country store, and Clinton would observe him often extending credit to those who couldn't afford their basic staples. In those humble surroundings, he learned to observe and listen and hone his relational skills gleaned from his grandfather. It was the lessons learned in his youth about community, education, racial equality, kindness, and reconciliation that ultimately shaped his "New Covenant." And he quickly observed that it was authentic relationships that would tell the story.

During his presidency, he developed and maintained many authentic relationships that also served his greater leadership goals. One of the relationships that became a beacon of goodwill was his friendship with Nelson Mandela. The iconic pictures of President Clinton with the former president of South Africa stand as just one illustration of his many international efforts, which included: the Middle East peace crisis, conflicts in Northern Ireland, the Mexican peso crisis, and the conflicts in Bosnia and Kosovo. At the end of his presidency, Clinton continued to develop relationships to support his end goals. When President George W. Bush took office, Clinton appealed to him to continue the federal government's support of AmeriCorps. President Bush not only agreed, he doubled the funding. Clinton's ability to make people feel like they mattered, whether friend or foe, allowed him to weave many characters into his story.

As a leader, when assessing communication and commitment to the people in your organization or under your leadership, it is important to reflect on the relational influences that thread through your life. In so doing, you can better understand how you relate to others, identify the knots that need to be untangled, and how to best harness those influences to support your story. Your life is always weaving a story, and understanding the arc of that narrative will strengthen your leadership and generate greater loyalty among your followers.

Plot Twists—Leaders Learn to Be Flexible in Their Story

Leaders also have to be prepared for plot twists as they put their personal philosophies into action. With his characters in place, President Polk set a course to annex the Oregon territory with the slogan "54/40 or fight." Polk's dream was to acquire land well into present-day Canada (up to the latitude line 54 degrees, 40 minutes), but he also understood that another war with Great Britain was not in the best interest of the country. Instead of the "fight," Polk was flexible and ultimately negotiated for the border we share with Canada today.

President Clinton also had to adjust his plot with health care reform. When the plan fell short, instead of throwing in the towel, the president returned to the drawing board to find a compromise to resurrect parts of the plan that would push towards the end goal. While there was no sweeping change by the end of his administration, there were significant advances in breast cancer research, HIV/AIDS advancements, and the creation of a Children's Health Insurance Program (CHIP).

Leaders will need to be flexible to change the tapestry of their stories and in some cases "tie knots" around sweeping agendas that are not effective, rethreading new ideas into the scene. This often requires the humility and ability to compromise, and a moving perspective, that keeps a watchful eye on the characters in the story.

Spoiler Alert—Leaders See the End Game

Many movies begin with a scene that depicts the end of the story. The viewer, while not fully aware of its meaning, has recognized that the ending will guide the entire plot. In the same way, when President Polk took office and clearly identified his endgame, the plot of his presidency revolved around his philosophical North Star. So also, President Clinton's New Covenant was the beacon that guided his efforts in—and out of—office. And, in hindsight, his direct successor—George W. Bush—became yet another character benefiting from both Polk's and Clinton's ability to see the endgame.

Gazing over the grieving masses in Oklahoma City in 1995, it was as if President Clinton had his eyes on the future presidency of Governor George W. Bush, who sat right below the podium in the front row. There sat a man who could only govern thanks to the endgame of President Polk, who secured his home state of Texas for the Union. And there also sat a leader who did not know at the time that his future presidency would require a similar moment at Ground Zero in New York City six years later. Surely, the words and wisdom of President Clinton from Oklahoma City shaped President Bush's own personal philosophical approach when he faced a nation in mourning.

During their presidencies, both #11 and #42 drove their "twenty-four hours of Le Mans" toward the finish line. Carving the corners and adjusting their speed, they were guided by a personal North Star in order to give others a better life story along with them. If Lee Iacocca were to name their tapestry, it would read "They Thought Like Ferrari."

For future leaders who want to prepare for the same driving test: Know your end game. Follow your North Star. Mind your bumpers. And manage your speed.

Chapter 3

George W. Bush & Harry S. Truman

Leaders Make Tough Decisions

*"Even if it's the wrong decision,
a quick decision is almost better than anything."*
–Eric Schmidt, former CEO of Google

*"Ladies and gentlemen, seldom has history offered
a greater opportunity to do so much for so many.
I ask the Congress to commit $15 billion
over the next five years … to turn the tide
against AIDS in the most afflicted nations
of Africa and the Caribbean."*
–George W. Bush

Fifteen years after the State of the Union address that announced PEPFAR—The President's Emergency Plan For AIDS Relief—former President George W. Bush cradled a baby in Namibia's Windhoek Central Hospital while its mother beamed nearby. As the infant reached out to touch the president's cheek, he realized that he held in his hands a living testimony of the nearly two million newborns that have been declared HIV free to infected mothers, thanks to his decision to fund the program during his presidency. At the time, his plan required convincing Congress—and American taxpayers—that their generosity would save millions of lives overseas, while an AIDS epidemic also lingered at home. In hindsight, that decision birthed a program that has eclipsed earlier estimates, saving seventeen million lives to date.

Not all bold decisions emanating from boardrooms and corner offices guarantee the satisfaction of realizing such profound success. Yet, for those in the decision-making seat, there is an understanding that satisfaction cannot be tied to an immediate outcome or popular opinion. In the words of President Harry Truman—another bold decision maker—"You have to wait for the dust to settle." For both President Bush and President Truman, the dust has settled over Africa and Europe, and millions of lives have risen from the ashes.

If the former presidents of the United States were to all enter their data into Match.com, there is little question that when it comes to bold decision-making, #33 Harry Truman and #43 George W. Bush would be a near perfect match for a dinner date. Although Truman would have probably lied about his height (five foot eight) and his education (no college) and Bush would have reached for the bill (privileged upbringing) while insisting on a paper-napkin Texas barbecue (he loved his cowboy image), their common interests in value-driven decision-making would fill the gap between the height and economic differential. The president who declared a war on terror and the president who authorized the atomic bomb would probably order a soft drink and a bourbon respectively, while unapologetically selecting exactly what they wanted off the menu. Two presidents markedly comfortable in their own skin would then unquestionably feast on discussions about the manna from heaven that was the Berlin Airlift and the nourishment that PEPFAR provided across a continent whose life expectancy was once age 20. And while Bush would reach for the bill, Truman would remind him that the "buck stops here."

Both President Bush and President Truman assumed office with tough acts to follow. Truman was bookended by FDR and Eisenhower, while Bush stepped into the shadow of his father, President George H.W. Bush. Yet, both leaders were undaunted, masterful at making swift, bold decisions as World War II came to a halt, and both the Cold War and the war on terror began to rise. History has shown that they both ordered a three-course meal of value-driven leadership, loyal staffing, and efficient decision-making. Consider yourself invited to their table, to share in the lessons they mastered during their administrations.

A CHARGE TO KEEP—LEADERS MAKE VALUE-BASED DECISIONS

The Irish poet Oscar Wilde wrote the popular phrase "life imitates art." You can learn a lot about a person by merely viewing the art that they choose to hang on their walls. When George W. Bush moved into the Oval Office, he brought his favorite painting, *A Charge to Keep,* which is the same name as his favorite Christian hymn. The western painting depicts a pioneer charging up a mountain on a horse with others behind—possibly in pursuit. It has been said that President Bush found his personal identity in that painting and in the words of the hymn:

A charge to keep I have,
A God to glorify,
A never dying soul to save,
And fit it for the sky.

To serve the present age,
My calling to fulfill:
O may it all my powers engage
To do my Master's will!
Arm me with jealous care,
As in Thy sight to live;
And O Thy servant, Lord, prepare
A strict account to give!
Help me to watch and pray,
And on Thyself rely,
Assured if I my trust betray,
I shall forever die

According to Bush's secretary of commerce, Don Evans, that hymn best sums up the man, George W. Bush. Holly Kuzmich, executive director of the George W. Bush Institute, said President Bush was always driven by his "charge to keep" and his core principles when he made decisions—principles he coined as "compassionate conservatism." Those principles include a sense of compassion, a priority on human freedom, the commitment to less government, and accountability to individual free will and personal responsibility. Bush deeply believed that

---

"To whom much is given, much will be required."

He had an unwavering belief that you can care about what's happening at home and care about people around the world at the same time. There was no greater illustration of his compassionate conservatism and these beliefs than the creation of the President's Emergency Plan for AIDS Relief (PEPFAR).

During the Bush presidency, the United Nations in conjunction with the World Health Organization, released a study documenting that thirty-six million people were living with AIDS, and that the epidemic had already claimed twenty-two million lives. AIDS had left over eleven million orphans in Africa alone. The president noted that "we have the power to help ... we must show leadership and share responsibility."[7] When he signed the Global AIDS Act, authorizing PEPFAR, the president created a program that has committed billions of American dollars to this global crisis.

Where money is committed globally, critics abound. Yet the president remained committed to his leadership values and was able to convince Congress to reauthorize the program in 2008 and double America's financial commitment. To date, over seventeen million lives have been saved and medication has helped prevent the spread of AIDS from mothers to their infant children, along with other programs. In the Bush Library and Museum, there is a display with personal gratitude letters exchanged between lead U2 singer and activist, Bono, and the president. Bono stood with the president on the initiative and publicly called his decision, "the kind of John Wayne 'get it done' mentality that the greatest health crisis in six hundred years demands." Senator Joe Biden also acknowledged, "His decision to launch this initiative was bold, and it was unexpected. I believe historians will regard it as his single finest hour." Many do.

Dr. Martin Luther King said, "A genuine leader is not a searcher for consensus but a molder of consensus." Leaders must learn to be "comfortable in their own skin" and confident enough to not compromise their values, nor ignore the decisions their values demand. In an age where social media has given voice to worldwide criticism at the micro level, there is no greater time to stand firm on values-based decision-making that helps mold consensus rather than seeking it.

Decisions that Help Others

President Harry Truman was no stranger to molding consensus rather than seeking it. On March 12, 1947, Truman gave a speech to

Congress, calling for economic support to counter Soviet expansion during the Cold War. Known as the Truman Doctrine, the president initiated a bold foreign policy underpinned by the same values echoed by President Bush decades later—assist free people to exert their own free will and care for both domestic and foreign need. He stated, "If we falter in our leadership, we may endanger the peace of the world, and we shall surely endanger the welfare of this nation." As a result, the Marshall Plan passed in 1948, supplying aid to Western Europe after World War II and was credited by Winston Churchill for "saving western civilization." Like President Truman, leaders must stand firmly on their values and never waver.

Bold, values-based decisions are best tested with challenges and one of the first, great challenges of the Cold War erupted in 1948. The Soviet forces deliberately blocked all access to Berlin, hoping to force the Western allies to retreat. At the time, Berlin had just over a month's supply of food and coal. Under the threat of a new war with the Soviets, Truman refused to back down, and instead devised a bold plan to airlift supplies into Berlin. For months, German civilians watched over six hundred flights a day deliver five thousand tons of food and fuel to the over two million people affected by the blockade. Truman was criticized for attempting the impossible, but his commitment to the people and the plan was unmovable. Finally, the Soviets lifted the blockade without initiating war.

> On May 12, 1949, the blockade ended: The lights of Berlin came on again. The airlift was over, after a year and two months, 277,804 flights, and the delivery of 2,325,809 tons of food and supplies. For Truman it was a momentous victory. Firmness and patience had prevailed without resorting to force. War had been averted.[8]

Any values-based decision will be met with criticism and challenge. Strong leaders must be resolute and prepared to stand firm on their underlying convictions. This is a serious "charge to keep." It is the art of charging up a hill, with critics in pursuit, and leading others into consensus on the journey. A true leader's life will imitate this art.

THE DREAM TEAM—BOLD DECISIONS REQUIRE SURROUNDING YOURSELF WITH GOOD PEOPLE

In August of 1992, the United States Olympic Men's Basketball Team won a gold medal by defeating Croatia 117-85. Dubbed the "Dream Team," this collection of eleven future Hall of Famers, wowed the world in what has been called the "greatest group of stars ever assembled on the same team in any sport."[9] Commenting on his team, Charles Barkley said, "Everybody in the world has an ego. The only difference between us is we have a reason to have an ego."

It is no easy decision to build a team of individuals who at any time may just eclipse your talents and abilities. To play alongside Charles Barkley requires enormous confidence that defies comparison. Yet to play alongside Charles Barkley secures a greater chance for victory. Leaders must first make the bold decision to hire good people, so that those good people can support their bold decisions. As I write, the news is reporting that a major world leader has encouraged his entire government to resign in an apparent effort to maintain personal power. While some have called this a "bold" decision, history has proven that coups are not bold—they are just brash. Unfortunately, this strategy is often echoed from boardrooms to break rooms to locker rooms when leaders believe that surrounding themselves with weaker people will eliminate threats to their power.

Both President Bush and President Truman prioritized surrounding themselves with good people who were talented, trustworthy, and sound advisors. They relied on these good people to help them make bold decisions in difficult situations. When Truman appointed George Marshall to the position of secretary of state, one of his advisors told him to think twice because people would come to recognize that Marshall would make a better president. Truman did not hesitate to agree with his advisor. He acknowledged that Marshall probably *would* make a better president but qualified that was precisely why he was chosen. He wanted the best people around him.

Credit Where Credit Is—or Isn't—Due

When Secretary of State George Marshall developed what became known as the "Marshall Plan" after World War II—fostering the creation of the North Atlantic Treaty Organization (NATO), President Truman did not hesitate to give Marshall the credit. Truman stated on more than one occasion that it was remarkable how much could be accomplished if you didn't care who received the credit. He was able to execute the bold decision to implement the Marshall Plan, because he had unwavering trust in his secretary of state and the self-confidence to allow him to do his job.

In his biography about Harry Truman, David McCullough writes:

> *There was no vast foreign policy machinery at the White House. There was no vast machinery on any subject at the White House … [And no one trying to] make their reputations by undercutting … by slitting the throat of a Secretary of State … by proving to the President, by trying to prove to the President, that they're smarter and more brilliant and their ideas are better [than the Secretary of State] … None of that existed. Had anybody at the White House tried to behave that way, he would have been out of there in thirty seconds flat. The loyalty of those around Truman was total and would never falter. In years to come not one member*

of the Truman White House would ever speak or write scathingly of him or belittle him in any fashion. There would be no vindictive "inside" books or articles written about this President by those who worked closest to him. They all thought the world of Harry Truman then and for the rest of their lives, and would welcome the chance to say so.[10]

The same could have been written about George Bush. Holly Kuzmich, who has worked for President George Bush for nearly twenty years, described how the president attracted and maintained such a talented and committed staff.

- He was not a micromanager, which made him a delight to work for while everyone knew they had to do their job well.
- He respected his staff and developed an amazingly loyal team.
- He created a culture that was hard-working and did not allow for infighting.

When Dick Cheney was tasked with finding George Bush a suitable vice-presidential candidate, Bush quickly recognized that Cheney himself was more than qualified. Cheney's political experience had far eclipsed Bush's—as a former United States Representative, former Chief of Staff for President Gerald Ford, and Secretary of Defense for his father—and Bush did not hesitate to select him. Bush believed Cheney could do the job better than any of the other candidates for the position and reportedly never regretted his decision.

According to Kuzmich, President Bush—while kind and compassionate—did not "suffer fools" and demanded disciplined, excellent work from his staff. He was confident in their abilities, and confident they would only approach him with very well thought out recommendations. Because his bold decision-making required air-tight research and support, he gave his staff the dignity of doing their jobs without micro-managing, but also did not tolerate lackluster preparation. Nor would he allow infighting. He was well aware that the casualties of a civil war could very well be the administration itself. In the same way, leaders must discern that bold decisions require even bolder recommendations. And infighting must be avoided at all costs.

Recently, I had a major decision to make as a leader. It was a decision that would radically change many aspects of our organization. I needed counsel from members and asked a group of twenty-five people to meet with me. I intentionally invited people from various backgrounds, perspectives, and points of view. I invited people who are always supportive as well as those who are rarely on board with new ideas. The decision was so important, I knew it would be a mistake if I loaded the group with "bobbleheads" who only said yes. By the end of the evening, there was strong consensus in favor of my proposed direction. But what made it strong was not the fact people agreed with me, it was the fact that people who normally disagree were on board. There was a spirit of unity among the group based on our love for our organization. I learned a powerful lesson that night that smart people with strong opinions can often make your decisions better. Don't let the fear of opposition, critics, and their criticism of your ideas keep you from making the best decision with the best team.

Many of us will never have the opportunity to assemble a team that includes Larry Bird, Magic Johnson, Michael Jordan, and Charles Barkley. Nor will we be faced with the challenge of rebuilding western society. Yet, no matter what our goals, potential dream-teamers abound if you are willing to seek out talent that can challenge and propel you and your vision towards bold decisions. To paraphrase Charles Barkley, there is nothing like the satisfaction of acknowledging "the only difference between our team is we have a reason to have *absolute confidence*."

RIGHT ON TIME—BOLD DECISION-MAKING REQUIRES EFFICIENCY

In 1519, the conquest of Mexico by Hernán Cortés was initiated and thus began the overthrow of Veracruz on Mexico's Gulf Coast. Cortés was well aware of the Aztec religious practice of human sacrifice and the horrific stories of beating hearts being removed to present to the Aztec gods. Therefore, one of his first military actions was to order the burning of his own ships once they reached shore to remove any option of retreat by his men. Once his decision was made to conquer, he did not leave room for second-guessing. Like Cortés, leaders need to make bold decisions and remove any opportunity for backtracking or interference.

According to biographer David McCullough, President Harry Truman was once asked by a reporter how he made decisions. "I ask advisors to study the situation and give opinions. Then I retire to my living quarters and spend hours going over papers and everything provided. Then I make the decision," Truman answered.

The reporter then asked, "What happens if you have made the wrong decision?"

"Then I make another decision," Truman responded.[11]

This discipline to make swift decisions and avoid second-guessing himself was essential to Truman's decision to drop the first atomic bomb. He had to act quickly to ensure the end of the war, and not look back. Essentially, he had to make the decision and "burn his boats."

High-velocity Decisions

With the surrender of Germany in World War II, Truman—who had just assumed office the day FDR died—was concerned about the cost of American soldiers' lives with an invasion of Japan. He was briefed on the top-secret work of the Manhattan Project and the successful test of the atomic bomb. He decided there was another way to formally end the war and preserve Allied lives. On the morning of August 6, 1945, a B-29 bomber called the Enola Gay flew over Hiroshima, Japan, and dropped the first atomic bomb on the city. Just two days later, Truman authorized a second atomic bomb on the city of Nagasaki. The destruction was so severe that the civilian casualties were estimated to be in the hundreds of thousands. Japan surrendered days later. The world would never be the same—propelling the United States into an arms race with the Soviet Union.

Many remain troubled by the decision. Yet Winston Churchill called it "the decision that was no decision." When asked to comment about his actions, Truman answered: "The final decision of where and when to use the atomic bomb was up to me. Let there be no mistake about it. I regarded the bomb as a military weapon and never had any doubt that it should be used. The top military advisers to the president recommended its use, and when I talked to Churchill he unhesitatingly told me that he favored the use of the atomic bomb if it might aid to end the war."[12]

And according to McCullough, "In years to come, Truman often said that having made his decision about the bomb, he went to bed and slept soundly. He would be pictured retiring for the night at the White House, his mind clear that he had done the right thing.[13]

Truman had weighed the options—the pros and cons—and made a decisive choice.

There is no bolder decision-making moment than when a leader is aware that the decision comes at great cost.

Many have been stalled in deliberations and indecision, afraid to assume responsibility and absorb the cost. And many have paid a greater price for this hesitation. The major drivers for hesitant decision-making are fear, the risk of conflict, and overthinking when not all the information is available. In order to make efficient, bold decisions, those fears must be met with resolution. Both Bush and Truman agreed that a swift decision does not require 100 percent of all the available data and analysis. Once enough information has been presented, they boldly made a choice.

In one of his letters to shareholders in the late 1990s, Jeff Bezos, CEO of Amazon, wrote about the importance of what he termed the "high-velocity" decision-making process at the company:

"Most decisions should probably be made with somewhere around 70 percent of the information you wish you had. If you wait for 90 percent, in most cases, you're probably being slow. Plus, either way, you need to be good at quickly recognizing and correcting bad decisions. If you're good at course correcting, being wrong may be less costly than you think, whereas being slow is going to be expensive for sure."[14]

Certainly, that philosophy has served Amazon well.

"The Decider"

One of President Bush's greatest strengths was his delegating and his swift decision-making based on concise recommendations from trusted staff. He preferred brief, well-crafted memos over lengthy policy documents and has been called the best one-minute manager to occupy the Oval Office. According to Wayne Slater, Austin bureau chief for the *Dallas Morning News*,

Rather than hear fifteen minutes of recommendations, he wants to hear a minute. And he wants to hear from a series of people, *What do you think? What do we do about this issue*? And he distills from those ideas what his decision is. And he makes a decision and moves on. I don't know of any case that I can remember where he's regretted the decision that he's made. He recognizes decisions were wrong, but he says, 'You have to make the decision based on what you think at the time.'[15]

As the United States faced a major financial crisis in 2008, President Bush turned to his secretary of the treasury, Hank Paulson, and sought his input. The government had just taken over Fannie Mae and Freddie Mac, Lehman Brothers was a ghost town, and the president was facing tough choices regarding using American tax dollars to fix a problem created by the few. After hearing Paulson's bold proposal, Ben Bernanke, chairman of the Federal Reserve, confirmed to the President that this was the worst financial crisis since the 1930s. In Bush's own words from his memoir, *Decision Points*: "His answer clarified the decision I faced: Did I want to be the president overseeing an economic calamity that could be worse than the Great Depression? ... As unfair as it was to use the American people's money to prevent a collapse for which they weren't responsible, it would be even more unfair to do nothing and leave them to suffer the consequences."[16]

That swift decision shaped the president's policies during the financial crisis.

Google It

In a 2017 episode of the podcast *Master of Scale*, former CEO of Google, Mark Schmidt, recounts the early days of the company, long before it was the behemoth it is today. He outlined their process for making swift decisions. "Google set up three meetings a week—one for staffing decisions, one for product decisions, and one for business decisions. If you had a proposal, you could bring it to that meeting and a decision would be made on it." He then recounted how the decision to purchase YouTube took only ten days. While Schmidt acquiesced that you cannot always avoid making wrong decisions, he did say that "even if it's the wrong decision, a quick decision is almost better than anything."[17]

It is a valuable practice to analyze the nature of your decision-making and evaluate its efficiency based on many of the principles modeled by presidents #33 and #43. Their commitment to quick decision-making based upon analysis, weighing the pros and cons, and refusing to look back may inspire you to "burn the boats" in your organization that are causing hesitation and retreat. President Bush and President Truman have proven that bold decisions require efficient and swift decisive action.

The Buck Stops Here

Collectively, the bold decisions during the presidencies of Harry S. Truman and George W. Bush have ushered the United States of America through some of its largest transitions. From World War II into the Cold War, from the tragedy of 9/11 into the war in Iraq, from the establishment of the United Nations, NATO, and the desegregation of the military, to the financial crisis of 2008 and the establishment of PEPFAR, there is no question their leadership required the ability to make bold decisions. And at the end of their dinner date with the nation, both were unwaveringly willing to pay the tab. The buck stopped there.

Chapter 4

Donald Trump & Andrew Jackson

Leaders Challenge the Status Quo

"If you are not going to divorce the status quo,
you will give birth to mediocrity."
–Israelmore Ayivor

"Last year, I heard through friends the story of Alice Johnson.
I was deeply moved. In 1997, Alice was sentenced to life
in prison as a first-time, nonviolent drug offender ...
Alice's story underscores the disparities and unfairness
that can exist in criminal sentencing—
and the need to remedy this injustice."
–President Donald Trump, State of the Union Address

O   n February 5, 2019, President Trump smiled at the upper
          tier of the House chambers as Alice Marie Johnson stood
          and acknowledged the thundering applause of Congress. Just
months earlier, she had celebrated her sixty-third birthday behind bars—
her twenty-first as a federal inmate. Smiling back at the commander in
chief—a president harshly criticized—Alice Marie did not hesitate to
show her admiration. In her own words: "I want to tell President Trump
that he has given me a second chance at life, and I am not going to blow
it. I am going to make President Trump so proud that he gave me that
chance in life to live again," Johnson said. "As I told someone else, it is
like being resurrected from the dead for me."[18]

For an African American grandmother released from a life sentence
by the presidential pardon provision, a resurrection from the dead by the
commander in chief nullified any criticism the pundits were throwing.
Surrounded by her family, she committed her undying support of the
president and personified the populist swell that placed President Trump
in office a few years prior.

The president issued an executive action that resonated profoundly
among more than two million incarcerated Americans, their families, and
a justice-prone public that was tuning in that night. President Trump
had, again, successfully diagnosed an American malady and championed
a social vaccine through the power of one. Prison reform became one of
the priorities of his administration. Like Andrew Jackson 200 years earlier,
the president had ridden roughshod through a populist swell of forgotten
Americans who felt imprisoned by their own injustices in the world's most
free society. And he had ridden all the way to the White House.

The Apprentice—Champion of the Common Man

If the seventh president—Andrew Jackson—had the opportunity to
host *The Apprentice*, there is no doubt that he would have selected con-
testant Donald Trump as his champion in challenging the status quo.

On set, Jackson may have first admired Trump's strikingly similar, flamboyant, reddish hairstyle—and with only a two-inch height differential they were almost eye to eye. He would have also noted that they stood shoulder to shoulder, ushering in the era of the common man with an often uncouth, rough-around-the-edges manner unafraid of an enemy duel. As the first populist president, Jackson had seized the reins from the Founding Fathers in 1828 and championed the Southerners who felt over-taxed by the Northern elitists. Similarly, Jackson would have admired Trump's ability to wrestle away a seemingly guaranteed election from Hillary Clinton and sound the bullhorn for the American Rust Belt two centuries later.

Both men had weathered personal scrutiny—Jackson facing the first presidential sex scandal, having married a woman not yet divorced—and Trump, twice divorced with a history of questionable innuendos towards women. Both wealthy and vocally critical of the political elite, Jackson's professional concern would have been Trump's career as a real estate mogul and his lack of public service or military involvement. Jackson, the hero of the Battle of New Orleans, a member of the House and Senate and a justice on the Tennessee Supreme Court, would have certainly questioned Trump's mettle as he viewed his resume somewhat politically deficient.

Could Trump withstand the public critics and put his words into action? Jackson, appreciating their uncanny commonality, would have readily tweeted his answer, "You're hired." To Jackson's relocation of the Native Americans and the Cherokee "trail of tears," he would have noted Trump's immigration policy and the building of the wall. Both vowed to clean up Washington, or as Trump campaigned upon, "drain the swamp." Jackson was called a *little Napoleon* and accused of "pimping for the Russian Tsar." Trump has been called a *dictator* and accused of coziness with Russia. Both have authorized their own biographies and neither makes apologies for their own portrayal. Yes, two centuries later, Trump the

Apprentice could withstand the same scrutiny and legacy as Jackson the populist to challenge the status quo.

Andrew Jackson #7 and Donald Trump #45 are unquestionably similar. Both were clearly their own man and were not afraid to stand up for what they believed and stand against any opposition. While criticisms about style, substance, and scandal abound, for leaders who are willing to listen, there is much to be learned from them and how they clearly defined what needed to change, charted a course, and took definitive action.

LEADERS CHALLENGE THE STATUS QUO BY CLEARLY DEFINING WHAT NEEDS TO CHANGE

After a surprising and resounding victory in 2016—a victory some consider one of the first third-party elections where Republican voters rejected the establishment for a reality TV star—President Trump made radical claims and demanded drastic change. He called for building a wall to stop the flow of illegal immigration on the border. He criticized the intelligence community, enacted executive orders to limit immigration, and advocated tariffs on Mexico and China, promising to recapture manufacturing jobs. He spoke of cutting taxes, destroying ISIS, repealing Obamacare, and fixing the criminal justice system. He may have been brash, but he was clear about the problems he had publicly committed to change. And he often invited others to the White House to ask questions and listened to concerns.

Leaders ask the right questions in order to define what needs to change.

On May 30, 2018, actress Kim Kardashian West arrived at the White House for a meeting with President Trump on behalf of inmate Alice Marie Johnson, who was celebrating her sixty-first birthday in prison that day. Kardashian had been scrolling through Twitter in 2017 and found the story about this great-grandmother who had spent the first twenty-one years of her life sentence in federal prison for a nonviolent drug offense. The injustice of the sentence, and the rehabilitative story told about Johnson, touched Kardashian and she vowed to help her cause. Aware of the president's pardon power and commitment to criminal justice reform, Kardashian communicated with the president's son-in-law who was leading the prison reform legislative effort and was able to secure the meeting. As a result of her appeal, the president granted clemency to Alice Marie just one week after meeting with Kardashian. For the first time in twenty-one years, Alice Marie Johnson was able to hold her children, grandchildren, and great-grandchildren outside prison walls.

The appearance of Alice Marie at the president's State of the Union Address early in 2019 provided the American public a poignant example of the dire need for prison reform and the president's commitment to doing what he had communicated—supporting a bipartisan legislative effort to get that done. Early in his administration, President Trump vowed to fix the broken prison system and reverse the damaging effects of the 1994 crime bill that set mandatory minimum sentences—often life sentences—for nonviolent drug offenders. He clearly communicated that the system was overcrowded and unjust, and that prior administrations had been unsuccessful in producing and passing any legislation to reverse the problems.

At the State of Union Address, he highlighted his recent signing of the First Step Act[19]—hailed the most impactful criminal justice reform legislation to have been passed in years. Alice Marie Johnson provided the living proof that the problem was real and the solution was life changing. President Trump had succeeded in leading a bipartisan effort to work together on a populist problem affecting many Americans and even his critics agreed. In the words of CNN commentator Van Jones, an ardent opponent of the president: "When you have formerly incarcerated people taking the lead, and law enforcement, and strong senators on both sides of the aisle … I think you have got to give him [President Trump] some credit."[20]

Like President Trump did with criminal justice reform, leaders who challenge the status quo must be willing to get out in front of an issue, clearly spell out what is wrong, and then sell the change to the organization.

Bank on It

One of the most convicting quotes by management expert and author Peter Drucker is: "Nothing is less productive than to make more efficient what should not be done at all." In leadership, we often find ourselves in a position of "spinning our wheels"—trying to prop up something that needs to be discontinued. For example, as the photography world began to shift to digital, Kodak found itself in that position and failed to completely diagnose the necessary changes. With unprecedented market share rallying American families around their "Kodak moments," its inability to adapt from film to digital saw Kodak's last moment sink on the ship of status quo. Kodak's leadership needed to consider total change or risk extinction. They received the latter. This scenario is one where history has been known to repeat itself.

Prior to the presidency of Andrew Jackson, the Second Bank of the United States was established under President Madison, initially in response to the need to finance the War of 1812 with Great Britain. The intention was to economically strengthen the federal government. When peace came, the plans for the bank were scrapped, but then a need for a more stable, uniform paper currency brought necessity of the bank back into focus. The bank was established in 1816 with a charter renewal set for twenty years later. The bank was owned by both the federal government and private investors and often suffered under poor management. When President Jackson assumed office, he vowed to abolish the bank altogether, calling it unconstitutional. Like Jefferson, Jackson believed that the government was only delegated powers which were specified in the constitution. He was also concerned about the lack of regulation and interference into state banks—many of which were managed by his friends. Ultimately, Jackson did not believe in paper money, but only in "specie"—silver or gold coins. When Congress passed a law to recharter the bank, Jackson vetoed the bill creating a "bank war" for his administration—a large issue in his reelection campaign. Once reelected, Jackson successfully "decentralized" and destroyed the bank by unilaterally requiring the money be drawn out to either settle the national debt or be dispersed to state banks. The Senate—led by Henry Clay—voted to censure Jackson for his unilateral actions, but Jackson refused to cooperate or turn over documents. In the end, Jackson prevailed—succeeding in measuring his options and taking bold action to ensure that the change endured. For sixteen years, the Bank of the United States had been the standard. Jackson saw another opportunity to upset the status quo. Leaders who challenge the status quo must often weigh the best options and consider total change.

LEADERS CHALLENGE THE STATUS QUO BY CHOREOGRAPHING CHANGE

In late 2005, Bob Iger assumed the role of Disney CEO and inherited a flagging animation department—the bedrock of the Disney organization. Instead of stepping into the shadow of his predecessor, Michael Eisner, Iger found himself overshadowed by Woody the toy cowboy and an astronaut named Buzz Lightyear. Pixar, the animation company owned by Steve Jobs's Apple, was the clear leader in animation at the time and had developed a strained relationship with Disney. Iger knew he needed to address the animation problems from the outset and decided to attempt the impossible—convince Steve Jobs to sell Pixar to Disney. They met, and Iger quickly realized the challenges of this deal far outdistanced its viability. Yet, he was more convinced than ever that this deal would resuscitate Disney animation and breathe new life into the organization. So, he charted a course to not only strengthen his relationship with Steve Jobs by a personal trip to Pixar headquarters, but also convince his board of directors that this idea was worth the expense. As the board readied its vote, Iger crossed the finish line with a rousing plea: "When animation soars, Disney soars. We have to do this. Our path to the future starts right here, tonight."[21] The board voted in favor of the acquisition and Disney animation has been transformed. Iger's careful combination of relationship building, strategic planning, and wise negotiation choreographed this monumental deal. The best way to change the status quo is not a result of improvisation. Leaders must carefully choreograph change by identifying a plan, a process, and the right people.

Self-interest Well Understood

In 1831, during the presidency of Andrew Jackson, French diplomat and historian Alexis de Tocqueville visited America to study the American prison system. During his travels in between prisons, Tocqueville visited with President Jackson at the White House. While not impressed by the president (to say the least), Tocqueville's journey inspired one of the more influential books of that century, *Democracy in America,* where he examined liberalism and equality. Among other observations, Tocqueville noted that Americans live by the principle of *self-interest rightly understood.* In other words, Americans partner together to further the interests of the group and, thereby, to serve their own interests. This regard for themselves often engenders patriotism and sacrifice of time and property for the greater good of all as well as personal reward.

Some assume, from his portrayal in the press, that President Trump is a stranger to anything *self-interested rightly understood,* and probably has not spent much time contemplating the writings of Tocqueville. But ironically, while standing under the banner "Make America Great Again," President Trump—the one who ultimately shook up the penal system that first brought Tocqueville to America—championed the cause of beleaguered believers of all faiths, committing his administration to take up the battle of religious liberty both domestically and worldwide. In the words of Johnnie Moore, one of the president's appointees on the United States Commission on International Religious Freedom, "America First never meant America Only" when it comes to Trump's commitment to religious freedom. Through this agenda, you can see President Trump bringing about change through a plan, a process, and putting the right people in place.

While controversial, the president has charted his plan and put the people in place with the authority and understanding to execute it. It has shaken up the status quo nationally, but also provided a new window into international religious freedom issues for all faiths at home and abroad. President Trump has tapped into *self-interest rightly understood* in order to advance changes in religious freedom. In turn, the president has received unprecedented, unwavering support from many aspects of the religious community—many of whom have languished under different levels of persecution worldwide.

When leaders see a need to shake up the status quo, they must put a plan in place to execute that vision. For Bob Iger, he realized he needed to meet with Jobs personally, keep his board informed and supportive, and cast a vision for the change. Similarly, President Trump identified an issue of religious liberty, surrounded himself with voices that were informed on the issue to advise him, then laid forth a plan to provide greater religious liberty to the oppressed. Both Bob Iger and President Trump followed a plan and a process to create a new normal to further the interests of their organization (Disney and the country) while also serving their personal leadership agendas. Leaders must harness the willingness and experience of people to join in the course of change.

I tend to frame this idea in terms of personal health. Every January 1, I join countless others in making commitments for the new year. One of my commitments always revolves around improving my health, particularly my waistline. The holidays always do their damage and by the start of the new year, I'm ready for a new me. What I have also discovered is if I don't partner with people on keeping true to my better health commitment, I will be sabotaged. I choose that word carefully because every year in the middle of January, these very sweet "terrorists" show up on my doorstep trying to persuade me to break my New Year's commitment to better health with Thin Mints, Do-si-dos, and Tagalongs. (You know who I'm talking about.) What I have discovered is if I want to change the status quo of my weight, I need partners to band with me to resist the temptation. So it is with most leadership roles. If you want to see change, you have to be willing to break with the status quo. Doing so is what separates leaders from followers. Followers always want to keep things the same. Leaders recognize that status quo is never really status quo. The more you try to keep it, the farther behind you will find yourself.

LEADERS CHALLENGE THE STATUS QUO BY TAKING ACTION

May 30, 2018, does not just mark the sixty-first birthday of former inmate Alice Marie Johnson celebrating the hope of new life, it is also the day—200 years earlier—that a future president violently ended the life of another.

While serving in the Senate and then as a lawyer and judge, Andrew Jackson developed a reputation for dueling to solve conflict. There are estimates that Jackson may have participated in up to one hundred duels. On May 30, 1806, Jackson and Charles Dickinson, a rival horse breeder who accused Jackson of cheating and insulting his wife, faced each other in a duel with pistols. Their *seconds*—the gentlemen chosen to ensure a fair and honorable fight—signaled and Dickinson fired, hitting Jackson in the chest. Jackson coolly compressed the wound with his hand, and was able to stand long enough to kill Dickinson with the next shot. Ironically, Jackson was never prosecuted for the murder—in fact, dueling was often considered a time-honored tradition. (Alexander Hamilton was killed in a duel with Aaron Burr just two years earlier.) Yet, he was accused of something worse than killing a man. Jackson was accused of violating the rules of engagement—firing his gun twice to ensure the death. Ironically, such behavior was out of place in these "affairs of honor." While Jackson—a self-avowed man of action—had defeated his foe, he was accused of failing to fully comply with the code of dueling. He proved his grit, but needed to temper his delivery. Killing a man was well within the rules. Breaking the code of conduct was way out of bounds. Leaders need grit to execute their plans, as well as a sense of discretion on proper delivery. One without the other leaves too much room for failure.

Think Over the Line, Not Outside the Box

You have probably heard it said that leaders *think outside the box.* While the sentiment of that statement is true, there is a larger reality that challenges that thinking. To think outside the box can be exciting and ripe with new discoveries. But for some organizations, this is not a practical reality. Suggesting a move to the fringe can be an untenable place. When challenging the status quo, this also can be a bridge too far.

I have attended many conferences where guest speakers discuss their organization. The reason they have been chosen to speak is because they are often doing something very unique. What I find, however, is if I attempt to apply their strategies in my environment, it falls flat. It is so outside my box, it actually serves as a detriment rather than ushering in progress. In fact, at times I've had to give myself permission to not feel guilty because I'm not doing what that highly creative speaker is doing in their setting.

A better way to challenge the status quo is to often think *over the line,* rather than outside the box. President Trump, in his promise to "drain the swamp," has often been checked by boundaries and limitations that cannot be circumvented. True change must first adhere to the existing framework, and then pressure can be applied to push past the status quo. For example, President Trump has frequently used the provision of executive order to *think over the line* to combat regulation on education, environmental issues, finance, and religious liberty. In the same way, leaders should challenge the status quo within the limits of reality. If wholesale change is needed in an organization, then outside the box may become the answer. But if pushing a team to a new level is the goal, *thinking over the line* is often the most effective approach. Where there exists a code of dueling, challenges often require operating within that code.

Thrilla in Manilla

On October 1, 1975, HBO's first pay-per-view boxing match was aired via satellite from Manila. Struggling to rebuild an international image after three years of martial law, Philippines president, Ferdinand Marcos, sponsored the event as a spectacle to distract from the tension his regime had caused. The heavyweight championship bout featured Muhammed Ali and Joe Frazier in their third and final fight. "It will be a killa and a thrilla and a chilla when I get the Gorilla in Manila," Ali chanted in his trademark, flamboyant style. He had his own agenda— to distract from the law that banned him from boxing and reclaim his title. Undoubtedly, Ferdinand Marcos was not the only one vying to maintain his image that day. And he would find, even a dictator was no match for Ali.

Called the "Louisville Lip," Ali grew up in Louisville, Kentucky, as Cassius Clay Jr. (named after a relative of the great politician Henry Clay). Ali was stripped of his boxing licenses after his refusal to serve in the army during the Vietnam War in 1967, and it was Joe Frazier who helped Ali through the tough financial years caused by his boxing ban. In 1971, the Supreme Court of the United States overturned the ruling and Ali returned to the boxing world a changed fighter. "The boxer that returned to the ring was different. Gone was the electrifying speed of the

Ali who was stripped of his titles and license to box in 1967, replaced by a post-1971 model that relied on grit, courage and wile."[22]

Ali reentered the boxing arena with a vengeance, relying on his thick skin, a lot of ego and the belief that he was the embodiment of his other nickname: "Greatest." Many thought he turned on his friend Joe Frazier with the relentless taunts, the competitive spirit, and the drive to win in Manila. For Ali, he simply, unapologetically, personified his nickname and displayed the thick skin that not only withstood the glove, but also the critics. Ali beat Joe Frazier by TKO in the fourteenth round, establishing himself as the leading heavyweight boxer of the twentieth century and the greatest in what has been called the "Golden Era of Heavyweights." Heavyweight boxing in the twentieth century is synonymous with the leadership of Muhammed Ali.

Perhaps no one has embodied the phrase "thick skin" like the man who could go fourteen rounds with Joe Frazier in the heat and humidity of the Philippines. But leave it to President Trump to throw his hat in the ring. On November 27, 2019, President Trump tweeted a picture of his head superimposed onto the body of Rocky Balboa.[23] In the midst of his reelection rallies, the impeachment process, and international tension, the president—literally—provided his image of a man willing to go all twelve rounds with Congress. The tweet exploded on social media, immediately igniting more than 330,000 likes and 100,000 retweets. Irrespective of opinion, any leader who has gone even a few rounds in a boardroom, conference room, or break room, knows that they must develop thick skin to challenge the status quo.

Born for the Storm

Nineteenth-century America hailed its own thick-skinned "Greatest" when Andrew Jackson was elected to the presidency. His presidency had such an impact on the country that the 1820s-1830s have been dubbed the "Age of Jackson." Orphaned at 15, Jackson's grit and determination, mixed with his brazen personality, drove his meteoric rise to the White House. His famous phrase reads like an Ali slogan: "I was born for the storm, and the calm does not suit me." To get things done, Jackson was unafraid to wrestle, box, or duel with either an enemy, the Congress, or, at times, within his own administration.

Beginning in 1828, Jackson faced a challenge that would come to define his second term in 1832—The Nullification Crisis. Facing off against the "Lexington Lip"—his nemesis, Kentucky Senator Henry Clay (yes, the one whose relative Ali was named after), Jackson went toe to toe over an issue of states rights.

The Nullification Crisis pitted the Southern states against the federal government's protective tariffs, which had been raised to 50 percent on foreign imports. The South took the biggest hit as a result of the tariffs, as they relied on foreign imports and exports. Vice President John C. Calhoun (of South Carolina) had previously declared the tariffs unconstitutional, pitting Jackson against his own vice president. Calhoun called for Southern states to ignore the federal law—thereby "nullifying" its existence in the South. Sensing the brewing conflict against the North and the South over the tariff crisis, Jackson sought to avoid civil war by battling against the state's perceived rights to nullify federal law. He isolated—and publicly humiliated—Calhoun, who, in 1832, became the first vice president to resign in American history.

But the crisis only intensified. Jackson railed against the South Carolina legislature for attempting to block the collection of revenues at its ports. He then lobbied Congress to further reduce the tariffs and directed his secretary of state to draft a document against nullification by attacking the constitutional theory of the South. Ironically, it was Henry Clay and John Calhoun (who had now been elected to the Senate) who wrote the bill called the "Compromise Tariff" that ended the crisis. Jackson did not hesitate to take the credit. He successfully averted a civil war, by going to war with his own vice president. Clearly, Jackson had challenged the status quo—internally and externally—and through thick-skinned grit, led the nation away from a greater crisis.

In a twist of history repeating itself, President Trump's acting attorney general, Matthew Whitaker, suggested in November 2018 that states have the right to nullify federal law but need the political courage to do so.[24] As they say, history has a way of repeating itself.

Floats Like a Butterfly, Stings Like a Bee

Within days of his inauguration, President Trump hung the portrait of Andrew Jackson in the Oval Office and visited his historic home in Tennessee. Playing the Jacksonian tune to his political base, Trump struck a chord with the common man—those disenfranchised by insider politics, big business, and the swampland upon which Congress is built. The populist who once paid Mike Tyson to box in Atlantic City laced up his boxing gloves, and like his predecessor, challenged the status quo from the moment he entered office. The apprentice had control of the boardroom.

For those like Alice Marie Johnson, who credits her freedom and new life to the president, he floats like a butterfly. For others, President Trump's policies, tweets, and entanglements sting like a bee. But like his predecessor, he will coolly compress his wounds as he duels to remain the last man standing.

The administrations of #7 and #45 endured the threat of a fourteen-round TKO in order to advance change. You may also find yourself up against the ropes on occasion, but true leaders are built to come back swinging.

Clearly define what needs to change, lay out your strategy, then take action.

You may often fight wounded, but keep in mind the difference you can make in the lives of others (like Alice Marie) and press on. For any leader who endeavors to challenge the status quo, that is the art of the duel.

Chapter 5

Theodore Roosevelt & Franklin Roosevelt

Leaders Instill Courage and Confidence

*"I learned that courage is not the absence of fear,
but the triumph over it."*
–Nelson Mandela

"You never lose until you actually give up."
–Mike Tyson

The young artillery officer stood in horror at the sight of the blood gushing down the president's left cheek. Staring in shock at the wound, he marveled at the joy on the president's face. Theodore Roosevelt leaned against the wall and untied his boxing gloves. Waving the young man off with his signature ear-to-ear grin, he probably muttered something about a great right hook before he was whisked away by his staff. That was his last boxing match—a hobby he had secretly arranged for years. As part of the *Fight Club* of the early 1900s, President Roosevelt had begun discreetly setting up boxing matches while he was New York Police Commissioner, often inviting professional fighters to participate. While governor of New York, he regularly sparred with trainers and staff. As president, his boxing days came to a halt when he took a right cross to the head, which left him blind in his left eye. Not to be deterred, he took up jujitsu. If there had been a UFC in 1933, he could have been the first president to qualify for a mixed martial arts match. Teddy Roosevelt was a competitor—physically, mentally, and politically.

A consummate promoter, had Teddy Roosevelt challenged his fifth cousin, Franklin D. Roosevelt, in an episode of *American Ninja Warrior*, they both would have navigated the gauntlet and emerged muddy, bloody, and exuberant—probably piggyback. While unmatched physically, they were both fearless competitors, well acquainted with limitations, relishing the challenge to prove their mettle more to themselves than anyone else. Both men would have been sponsored by the government—Teddy sporting a "Square Deal" logo and FDR wearing his "New Deal" slogan across his chest. Both would have carried America on their shoulders, hoisting others to safety and victory thanks to their government sponsorship. Most of all, neither would give up—Teddy "treading lightly and carrying a big stick" and FDR "fearing nothing but fear itself." Between Teddy's seven children and Franklin's six, they raised many warriors—four sons each who were trained to fight the battles endorsed by their fathers, serving valiantly in World War I and World War II respectively. Theodore Roosevelt and Franklin Roosevelt were well bred—and breeders—of courage and confidence. Trained on a battlefield of personal loss, they both paid a great price to pass this example to future generations.

Franklin, a healthy child of privilege, suffered from the effects of polio later in life, losing most of the function of his legs. In that trial, he learned the art of "lifting others up" through the daily challenge of hoisting his own body from a wheelchair. Teddy, a sickly child who endured ongoing challenges, eventually lost his first wife and mother and struggled to function without them. Through that trial, he learned the art of resiliency and the physical commitment to keep moving forward as a rancher, Rough Rider, and public servant. Courage and confidence, for both men, were born out of great adversity, and while they hailed from different political parties and different upbringings, both developed a strong will to lead America through the trials of expansive industrialization and the debilitating Great Depression. For leaders, the presidencies of #26 and #32 draw us into an arena of struggle, commitment, resiliency, strife, risk, valor, and joy—the mixed martial arts of courage.

GOOD GRIEF—COURAGEOUS LEADERS TRANSFORM DIFFICULTIES INTO OPPORTUNITIES

When surfer Bethany Hamilton lost her left arm in a terrifying shark attack at age thirteen, she addressed her fear and loss in an unmistakable act of courage—she stepped back on her surfboard one month later. After that first step of confidence, she did not look back, winning first place in the Explorer Women's Division of the NSSA National Championships just two years later. In her book, *Soul Surfer*, she wrote: "Courage, sacrifice, determination, commitment, toughness, heart, talent, guts. That's what little girls are made of; the heck with sugar and spice."[25]

She learned very young that suffering is the breeding ground for tremendous courage and enables the spice of life.

Rough Riders

"The light has gone out of my life," Teddy Roosevelt wrote in his journal on Valentine's Day 1884. In one terrible moment, his life completely changed. After receiving the wonderful news his wife had delivered a baby

girl on the birthday of his hero, Abraham Lincoln, Roosevelt received an urgent telegram to return home quickly. His wife was dying of a previously undiagnosed kidney disease. Rushing back to New York City from Albany, he was shocked to discover his mother had died that same morning of typhoid at age forty-eight. Just a few hours later, in the same house, his wife of four years stepped into eternity. Roosevelt was twenty-five, widowed, and the single parent of a newborn daughter. *"Black care rarely sits behind a rider whose pace is fast enough,"* he recorded soon after. In other words, sadness and depression cannot catch you if you keep moving and stay ahead of it. Determined to recover by pursuing challenge and adventure—physically and mentally—this became his antidote for grief. Once bowed by loss, he took up ranching, wrangling, hunting, traveling, military conquests, public and political service, ultimately transforming himself into a moving target of exuberance. Whether on the back of the horse on his ranch in North Dakota, leading a charge up San Juan Hill with fellow Rough Riders in the Spanish American War, or governing behind a desk, Theodore Roosevelt embodied courage and confidence in every form.

Marrying again, Theodore was blessed with five children who joined his daughter, Alice. His relentless energy propelled him into confident service to both the community and his presidency. He served as police commissioner and ultimately was nominated to be vice president under William McKinley. Threatened by his charisma, his political adversaries within his party relished the idea that the vice presidency would be a career-ending move for Roosevelt. However, they were shocked, as was the nation, when McKinley was assassinated and TR became president.

President Roosevelt confidently used his bully pulpit to bring his "Square Deal" to his domestic policy—which carried the United States into the industrial age. Called his three "Cs": *conservation* of natural resources, *control* of corporations, and *consumer* protection, he established national parks, challenged corporations, and went to bat for consumers. Supporting the Pure Food and Drug Act, Meat Inspection Act, and Elkins Act—to name a few—it was apparent the president was in tune with the painful trigger points suffered by the common man. His appreciation for nature and consumer protection ultimately led to the creation of our National Park System and the Food and Drug Administration. President Bill Clinton wrote:

> *"Teddy Roosevelt was the first president to come to grips with the challenges presented by America's transition from a rural to an urban society; from an agricultural to an industrial economy; from a fairly stable and homogeneous nation to a more dynamic, diverse one of new immigrants; from a nation of modest influence to a global power."*[26]

Since 2015, the great state of Texas has been governed by Greg Abbott. While known for his achievements in office, Abbott is also recognized as governing from a wheelchair. As a young law school graduate, Abbott decided to take a break from his preparation for the bar exam and go for a run. Little did he know how life-changing that one decision would become. While on that run, an old oak tree suddenly gave way and fell upon the young runner. Permanently paralyzed from the waist down, Abbott knew in that hospital that the rest of his life would require perseverance, determination, and a spirit that overcomes. The two steel rods placed in his back now serve as a daily reminder of the "steel spine" needed to rise above difficulty and show courage in the face of disaster.

Like Teddy Roosevelt, Governor Abbott faced tremendous difficulties but allowed that hurt to be transformed into even more courageous forms of service and leadership.

Strategic Alliances

Like his cousin twenty-five years earlier, FDR was humbled by his trials. After contracting polio at thirty-nine, he was determined to model the same courage for the nation as it took for him to get up in the morning and face another day. Ultimately confined to a wheelchair, FDR refused to let his illness hinder him and also fought to keep the public from being aware of his disease. Yet no one stood taller from a sitting position than FDR. Winston Churchill once commented: "Meeting Franklin Roosevelt was like opening your first bottle of champagne; knowing him was like drinking it."

As president, he inherited an economy in the midst of a great depression—faced with an unemployment rate of 26.3 percent compared to today's of less than 4 percent. Knowing he must act quickly and instill confidence in the nation, FDR set clear goals for his first one hundred days in office. This included passage of a "New Deal"— programs, public work projects, and financial reforms in response to the needs that arose from the Great Depression. The three "Rs" of the New Deal were: *relief, recovery, and reform*. As a result, FDR's support of the Banking and Securities Acts, among other programs, has been credited for saving capitalism, while his Social Security Act and the creation of FEMA brought calm to a shell-shocked public afraid of another financial downturn. Those government policies filtered down from Wall Street to Main Street very quickly. My paternal grandfather, all the days of his life, used to say, "FDR put shoes on my feet when I had none." These programs provided a thoughtful answer to public fear with clarity and certainty.

There was, however, more to fear than domestic troubles. The Nazi empire was mobilizing in Europe, and Japan was threatening the Pacific. Rising to the challenge after the "day that will live infamy," FDR forged a courageous alliance with Russia and Great Britain in order to conquer the opposing Axis Powers. FDR was keenly aware battles are not always meant to be fought alone and partnering with strategic allies can greatly increase the chance for success. Joining arms with a struggling Great Britain was not easy but FDR believed in Churchill and the importance of this long-time ally. However, embracing the Soviet Union and the ever-deceptive Stalin required forethought, risk, and ultimately a strategic decision. Throughout his four terms—the longest of any president—FDR demonstrated the willingness to take courageous risks and forge progressive alliances to move the country forward.

Recently, Apple announced a strategic partnership with Goldman Sachs and Mastercard to advance into new avenues of profitability. Rolling out a new credit card—called the "Apple Card"—this new initiative is projected to increase sales in Apple's services divisions and reach new consumer markets. For all three companies, leveraging each other's market share will increase the business platform of each organization and further their unique business goals.

According to the Corporate Financial Institute, the value in creating strategic alliances transcends breeding confidence in both parties. It also improves current operations, changes the competitive environment, fosters learning between partners, and provides cost and risk sharing. [27] These were among the values that motivated the Roosevelts to forge alliances as a tool to instill confidence in their programs as well.

Both Teddy and FDR embraced a robust life of courage and confidence by overcoming pain and opening their minds to new alliances and opportunities. Their ninja-like ability to cut through problems and navigate the country out of the quagmire is unmatched. In order to be fit for the demands of their calling, both presidents were strengthened through trials and faced their challenges head-on.

What is equally remarkable is they were able to do so with joy. Teddy Roosevelt—a man who endured much pain in his early life—most often sported an ear-to-ear grin in his photographs. The president who once said "comparison is the thief of joy" was truly beyond compare, remembered as a man of great courage and the embodiment of joy. Near the end of his life, he remarked how fulfilling his journeys had been at every stage, while learning contentment in trials and triumphs.

Franklin Roosevelt, in spite of a debilitating handicap, showed strength when navigating the country through great trial and peril. Remaining steadfast and approachable, his efforts invited joy to peek through the clouds of the Great Depression and the Second World War. Uninhibited by physical limitation, he discovered that "Happiness lies in the joy of achievement and the thrill of creative effort."

The leader who stands in the arena inspiring confidence and courage in others may uncover a more valuable trophy—overcoming struggle is often rewarded by a ready grin of joy.

THE ULTIMATE SIX-PACK: LEADERS BUILD MUSCLE WITH SIX TYPES OF COURAGE

Aristotle called courage the first virtue because it makes all of the other virtues possible. Taking risks is an inherent part of leadership. If you are not taking some levels of risk, chances are you are not really leading but simply managing and keeping your organization safe. There is a place in society for safety, but "the man in the arena" will not settle for safe.

But in order to take risks, leaders must act with courage.

Courage does not always move linearly but is multifaceted in how it manifests itself. Understanding the different acts of courage allows the leader to stretch their abilities in multiple settings. Below are six types of courage leaders should have in their arsenal as they face trials in many arenas.

1. Physical Courage

Courage is often identified with physical action. It is this type of courage that says I will jump in front of an oncoming bus to save my child. It is the courage of those aboard Flight 93 that stormed the cockpit on that terrible September morning. It is displayed on battlefields (much like TR on San Juan Hill) or by first responders. Physical courage involves strength that comes from within but risks bodily harm or even death. "Only those are fit to live who do not fear to die," said TR. Yet while physical courage is probably most familiar, it is also the most uncommon. Most people do not face situations in life that require great physical courage.

While running for his third term as president, Theodore Roosevelt was shot in the chest while giving a stump speech. Ever the driven politician, he continued his speech for an hour before going to the hospital. Fervent about his ideas and direction for the United States, Roosevelt risked physical setbacks to continue his fight.

2. Social Courage

Social courage is a willingness to stand firm in the midst of disapproval. It is remaining confident and comfortable in your own skin, completely unaffected by peer pressure. Leaders who are socially courageous understand who they are, how they are wired, and what they are created to do. It is the wisdom to know when to speak and when to stay silent. Winston Churchill said, "Courage is what it takes to stand up and speak; courage is also what it takes to sit down and listen."

Once, a retiring CEO at General Motors was asked to reveal the identity of his successor. The outgoing CEO responded, "That guy in Denver I had that big fight with last year." The other top executives wondered why they were not selected. The CEO explained, "He has his own opinions and is not afraid to voice them. You are all *yes men,* which is nice as number two, but lacking in skill to really lead. You'd all try to please rather than set direction."[28] Social courage is the ability to speak objectively, and then remain impervious to criticism and collective reasoning.

3. Intellectual Courage

Initiated by the presidency of Theodore Roosevelt, the United States has been transformed from an agrarian society to an industrial economy—to a pioneer in a worldwide technological revolution. Organizations and individuals that have refused to adapt have become roadkill on the information superhighway. Leaders must demonstrate intellectual courage to engage in thought-provoking ideas, consider revolutionary ways of doing business, and discontinue practices that are no longer viable. Intellectual courage requires risk in order to reap the reward. Think of Galileo standing before his interrogators in 1633 telling them the Earth revolves around the sun. He was sentenced to life imprisonment for his controversial views. Yet science was ultimately transformed.

To this day, the public has debated about the long-term impact of the New Deal. Critics are sharply divided, and FDR's programs have been subjected to mixed praise and criticism for the last eighty years. FDR was facing the challenge of leading America through the worst financial crisis at the time, and the bloodiest war of the twentieth century. Known as the "alphabet agencies," FDR championed the establishment of over one hundred government offices to address public need. He then turned his attention to Hitler. According to James McGregor Burns, author of *Roosevelt, The Lion and the Fox*:

> During the war years, Roosevelt became interested in Kierke-gaard, and this was not surprising. The Danish theologian, with his emphasis on man's natural sinfulness, helped explain to him, Roosevelt said, why the Nazis "are human yet they behave like demons." From Peabody homilies to Kierkegaard's realities, from the world of Hyde Park to the world of Hitler, the way was long and tortuous; the fact that Roosevelt could traverse that road so surely, with so little impairment to his loftiest ideals, and with such courage and good humor, was the final and true test of the man.[29]

The intellectual courage of FDR empowered him as a leader to think boldly in the face of tremendous financial crisis as well as the evils of totalitarianism.

4. Moral Courage

What is moral courage? Simply put, it is the willingness to take a stand for something. It is the courage to say "that is wrong" and to point to what is right. It is leadership that risks being mocked and ridiculed, put on probation or fired, and in some parts of the world could mean death. Willingness to stand for what is right often requires great moral fortitude.

It was this courage that prompted FDR to declare war on Japan after the bombing of Pearl Harbor. In speaking to Congress the day after "the date which will live in infamy," the president said: "No matter how long it may take us to overcome this premeditated invasion, the American people in their righteous might will win through to absolute victory. I believe I interpret the will of the Congress and of the people when I assert that we will not only defend ourselves to the uttermost but will make very certain that this form of treachery shall never endanger us again."[30]

This courage is rooted in ethics and integrity, values and beliefs. It was moral courage that caused FDR to not only stand up to the empire of Japan but also the bully of the European schoolyard, Adolf Hitler. Moral courage requires resolution to do what must be done and speaking soundly for what is right.

5. Emotional Courage

Psychology Today defines emotional courage as "a brief moment, a pivotal instant in time in which we take an action—we choose to heed our convictions, beliefs, and intentions and do what we know in our heads is good for us (instead of heeding our fears and anxieties and continuing to avoid the situation)."[31] Emotional courage demands an openness to being vulnerable in an age when vulnerability is viewed as weakness. Leaders who embrace vulnerability can impress a remarkable impact on their team.

Research professor and popular speaker Brené Brown has spent her life studying vulnerability. Her TED Talk, "The Power of Vulnerability," has garnered over twelve million views. In her words, "Vulnerability sounds like truth and feels like courage. Truth and courage are not always comfortable, but they're never weakness."

Emotional courage is the ability to be truthful in connecting emotionally with others, and courageous enough to be transparent. On April 23, 1910—the year after leaving office—Theodore Roosevelt stood before 2,000 people at the Sarbonne in Paris and delivered his most famous and emotionally charged speech. Quoted often by Brene' Brown in her presentations, it could be considered the original TED Talk, long before its time. His speech has become known as "The Man in the Arena," and has been widely quoted by leaders such as Nixon and Mandela—even tattooed on the arms of Miley Cyrus and Liam Hemsworth.

> *It is not the critic who counts; not the man who points out how the strong man stumbles, or where the doer of deeds could have done them better. The credit belongs to the man who is actually in the arena, whose face is marred by dust and sweat and blood; who strives valiantly; who errs, who comes short again and again, because there is no effort without error and shortcoming; but who does actually strive to do the deeds; who knows great enthusiasms, the great devotions; who spends himself in a worthy cause; who at the best knows in the end the triumph of high achievement, and who at the worst, if he fails, at least fails while daring greatly, so that his place shall never be with those cold and timid souls who neither know victory nor defeat.*

–Theodore Roosevelt

When the Washington Nationals faced the St. Louis Cardinals in the 2012 National League Division Series, player Mark DeRosa read part of Roosevelt's speech aloud to his teammates. James Wagner of the Washington Post writes, "Since his days at the University of Pennsylvania,

DeRosa would turn to those words before big games. This time, he felt he needed to share them ... Players who weren't in the clubhouse came streaming in ... DeRosa felt that his teammates, composed mainly of young players new to this stage, needed to hear something."[32]

And you may need to read that speech again and again. Sometimes those words of Teddy Roosevelt are exactly what is needed to bolster your courage and step into the arena.

6. **Spiritual Courage**

Spiritual courage is the expression of grappling with questions of faith and the meaning of life. It calls on leaders to seek answers and find purpose. Because one of mankind's greatest fears is death, wrestling with eternal, existential questions requires a commitment to face ultimate fear. Leaders often have had to guide the nation during times of great loss and make sense of death and tragedy.

For both Roosevelts, their tenure as president included times of war—a time where death was a threat for young soldiers, even in their own families. They were both called upon to demonstrate spiritual courage in the face of opposition and fear—especially when they sent their own sons to the battlefield. The fact that they did not spare their own children, but trusted their outcomes to an eternal perspective, gave confidence and courage to a nation also faced with those gut-wrenching realities of life and death.

Good leaders will make sure they are leveraging all six forms of courage on their leadership palette to respond to the differing needs of each situation. This is true not just for you as leader but also for recognizing and rewarding your team as they demonstrate courage.

BUILD-A-BEAR: LEADERS INSTILL CONFIDENCE AND SECURITY

President Theodore Roosevelt was not just an environmentalist, he was also an avid hunter—once authoring a book on the sport,

Hunting Trips of a Ranchman. It was, in fact, criticism of his book that prompted his environmental efforts. On one occasion in 1902, the president was invited to join a bear hunt in Mississippi. The president was not successful on the hunt, so his guide tracked a large bear with hunting dogs, clubbed it over the head, and tied it to a tree. The president, who was then summoned to kill the bear, refused and instead asked that the bear be put out of its misery by others while he turned his back on the scene.

Inspired by the story, a Washington Post political cartoonist drew a caricature of the encounter, which became wildly popular. Store owners in New York City were intrigued by the cartoon and quickly manufactured stuffed bears for their shop called "Teddy's Bear." This early 1900s fad ultimately became a worldwide phenom, and Teddy Bears still bring comfort and security to people of all ages today.

While you are not going to be a human teddy bear, as a leader, you are often sought out to bring comfort and security to your followers. You're the leader and they believe in you. But what do you do when you face a fearful situation? When your team is looking to you to see how to respond? Moments like these demand courage and confidence from you. In order to instill confidence, leaders must project confidence. That is where you need the visual of a duck. If you ever watch a duck on the water, it is peaceful and serene. Seemingly without effort, ducks gently glide across the water moving forward through the soft waves. If you looked at that same duck from underwater, you would see a much different scene. While that duck serenely glides across the waves, underneath he's kicking his little webbed feet like crazy. Above the surface there is calm even though below the water, there is a struggle taking place. So it is with leadership. Underneath what others can see, you may be fighting against the current and your world may be anything but serene. But above the waves, in view of your followers, they need the confidence and calm of a leader in charge.

A great example of this principle is the image of George W. Bush on September 11, 2001, sitting in the school classroom when Andy Card whispers in his ear, "Mr. President, we are under attack." President Bush instinctively knew the nation did not need to see panic but needed the calm assurance of the commander in chief. That calm assurance was modeled by a former president, and even though he was sitting in front of a classroom, he contained his anxiety and communicated confidence.

As a pastor, I'm often called into crisis situations. I'm not there to be the police or paramedic. My role is to bring encouragement, support, and faith into the middle of the storm that is raging around a family. I have learned over the years that one of the best actions I can take in those circumstances is to be a voice of calm and an arm of assurance. What I mean is I speak calmly and put my arm around the person who is in crisis. They are the ones whose loved one is in the ER, or they have received some terrible news, or the stability of their home has just been rocked to its core. In those moments, they don't need more chaos and panic, nor do they need every story of mine about a similar experience that may or may not have turned out so well. What they need is a calming voice, a confident hope, and an arm around them that communicates assurance. That is the role of pastors, but in reality, it's the role of every leader. In the midst of crisis and chaos, leaders must communicate calm, hope, and assurance that all will be okay.

Fireside Chatrooms

In order to instill confidence and security, leaders need to communicate with frequency and clarity. They also need to understand and utilize tools and tactics of communication that are personable, nonthreatening, and demonstrate the ability to identify with the listener.

FDR's speech to Congress on December 8, 1941, was given while a nation was frozen in shock. Just twenty-four hours earlier, the Japanese had devastated the Pacific fleet at Pearl Harbor in a surprise attack that took the lives of many servicemen and women. His carefully crafted speech delivered the facts in a clear and concise manner, expressing confidence in the military might of the United States, and communicating words of hope even in the face of imminent war. FDR demonstrated courage and confidence, inspiring both Congress and the American people to take action as he led the nation into the Second World War.

Yet, his most brilliant acts of inspiration were his unique "Fireside Chats." Informal, personable, and warm, the nation felt like they were offered a seat by the fire in the president's living room to discuss what was on their mind. In a series of thirty radio speeches broadcast between March 1933 and June 1944, the president spoke directly into the living room of homes across the nation. He shared his thoughts on a variety of topics ranging from the banking crisis to national defense. It is estimated 90 percent of Americans owned a radio and FDR understood the power of mass media. He began many of the addresses with the words "My friends," and often employed the words "you" and "I" to show the connection he had with the American people. Because the president regularly "came into their homes," the nation felt they knew the president and could trust what he would do for them.

In his first address, Roosevelt attempted to stop the "run on the banks" by declaring a four-day banking holiday and giving his first Fireside Chat to discuss the banking problem in a personable and understandable manner. With his signature warmth and charisma, he began: "My friends, I want to talk for a few minutes with the people of the United States about banking—to talk with the comparatively few who understand the mechanics of banking, but more particularly with the overwhelming majority of you who use banks for the making of deposits and the drawing of checks. I want to tell you what has been done in the last few days, and why it was done, and what the next steps are going to be ..."[33]

Confidence was instilled by a leader who carefully identified the problem and provided the steps that would be taken toward a solution. Security was instilled by the comfortable means of communication, and the warmth of expression. Leaders, whether facing crisis or in times of "business as usual," need to explore tools to comfortably and confidently communicate within their organization to facilitate an environment of productivity and trust. You may not gather your team around the fireplace, but they need to occasionally hear words from you that will give them a sense of calm and comfort. People work best in calm, cool environments, and as the leader, you set the temperature in the room. Confidence leads to greater productivity.

Into the Arena

Teddy Roosevelt—a man who endured much pain in his early life—most often sported an ear-to-ear grin in his photographs. The president who once said "Comparison is the thief of joy" was truly beyond compare, remembered as a man of great courage and the embodiment of joy. Near the end of his life, he remarked with satisfaction about the contentment he discovered through the trials and triumphs of life's journey. If life was his schoolmaster, he graduated with honors.

Franklin Roosevelt, in spite of a debilitating handicap, stood tallest when navigating the country through great trial and peril. Remaining steadfast and approachable, his efforts invited joy to peek through the clouds of the Great Depression and the Second World War. Uninhibited by physical limitation, he too discovered contentment and that "Happiness lies in the joy of achievement and the thrill of creative effort." When his fire was extinguished, the memory of his Fireside Chats lingered to warm the nation.

The leader who stands in the arena inspiring confidence and courage in others may uncover a more valuable trophy—overcoming struggle is often rewarded by the diploma of contentment and the ear-to-ear grin of joy.

Join the Fight Club. Tighten the six-pack. Bolster your confidence. And step into the arena.

Chapter 6

George H. W. Bush & Ulysses S. Grant

Leaders Invest in Relationships

*"The only thing that really matters in life
are your relationships to other people."*
–Dr. George Valliant, Director of the Harvard Grant Study

*"Dear Timothy: I want to be your new pen pal.
I live in Texas—I will write you from time to time—Good Luck."*
–G. Walker

Throughout his life, President George H. W. Bush—or "41" as he's been dubbed— ceaselessly pursued relationships. He was uniquely able to relate with people of all ages, ethnicities, socio-economic status, or gender. Using the pseudonym "G. Walker," the president even anonymously sponsored a child named Timothy in the Philippines until his death at age ninety-four. His handwritten letters join thousands of missives he penned over the years to maintain and build relationships.

In 1937, a researcher at Harvard University began a formal study of the factors that contribute to human well-being and happiness. The research team selected 268 male Harvard students who have been subsequently observed for seventy-two years. Over seven decades, the scientists developed a comprehensive viewpoint on what has affected the level of health and happiness of these men over a lifetime. In 2008, the director, Dr. George Vaillant, was asked what he had learned about human health and happiness. His response was breathtakingly simple: "The only thing that really matters in life are your relationships to other people."

President George H. W. Bush was a leader who understood the power, significance, and humanity of pursuing and cultivating relationships. His relational prowess led the nation through the Gulf War crisis, the fall of the Berlin Wall and end of the Cold War, the savings and loan crisis, and strengthened relations with China following the Tiananmen Square massacre. He was known for his extensive contact list and his unmatched diplomacy and decency. Juggling relationships with Russia, China, Europe, and a coalition of leaders in the Middle East, Bush successfully leveraged the most difficult relationships to hasten peace and cooperation across the globe.

Where "41" mastered the art of relationship building, his predecessor of a century and a quarter, Ulysses S. Grant (or "18"), was largely measured by his relational mishaps as president. Although his rise was meteoric in nature (when the war began in 1860, Grant was working in his family's store and by the end of the decade he was President of the United States), Grant's time as president dulled his stellar resume as a general and reputation as a man of highest integrity. Until famed biographer Ron Chernow recently recast Grant in a more favorable light, the decorated Civil War Union general turned president was largely known for the scandalous relationships in his administration and his weakened ability to govern due to nepotism and naïve loyalty to colleagues. In fact, the term "lobbyist" was first coined to describe the patrons who would drop by the Willard Hotel to influence Grant, while he habitually lounged in the lobby smoking cigars.

Somewhat similar in looks to the actor Leonardo DiCaprio, *Grant* will be produced by DiCaprio in a Steven Spielberg biopic based on Chernow's book. Ironically, the relational scandals in Grant's presidency could also borrow from DiCaprio's former movie titles: *The Wolf of Wall Street* could star Grant's brother-in-law who manipulated Grant during the gold panic of Black Friday 1869; *The Departed* could feature Grant's deposed secretary, Orville Babcock, and his involvement in the fraudulent Whiskey Ring; and *Titanic* could be headlined by his son Jesse's financial firm that squandered all of Grant's personal savings and sunk his finances at the end of his life. Grant was never personally charged with wrongdoing nor benefited from the many scandals he endured, but his deficit in character judgment and relationship management ultimately hindered his leadership. By the end of his eight years in office, each of his executive offices had come under Congressional investigation.

Where Bush could have been the protagonist in DiCaprio's *Catch Me If You Can*—with his far-reaching relational skills, Grant's inability to properly leverage relationships and set boundaries distanced him from his party and culminated in his decision to not seek a third term. (The 27th Amendment prohibiting more than a two-term presidency was not enacted until 1951.) In this chapter, the contrasting relational styles and stories of "41" and "18" provide both an Oscar-worthy feature film and a cautionary tale about the critical leadership skill of building and cultivating relationships—"the only thing that really matters in life."

LEADERS CULTIVATE EMPATHETIC RELATIONSHIPS

In its *Army Field Manual on Leader Development*, the United States Army incorporates empathetic relationship building as a core essential of its training. Clearly, building these relationships is a strategic leadership skill, not to be confused with weakness or malleability.

What is an empathetic leader? Simply put, it is a leader who understands and recognizes the feelings, opinions, and perspectives of others.

As the youngest pilot and aerial photographer for the U.S. Navy in World War II, George Bush was also assigned the task of censoring the outgoing mail the soldiers were sending their loved ones. His assignment required that he read each letter to ensure no sensitive material was inadvertently included by the officers. It was through reading these personal letters penned to mothers and girlfriends and wives that the president honed his empathy for others. He viewed his comrades through new eyes as he was granted access to their innermost thoughts, fears, joys, pains, and the longing for relationships back home.

His empathetic insight and ability to connect with people inspired his post White House Chief of Staff, Jean Becker, to call him the "tumbleweed." If you are not from the Southwest, that image may be somewhat lost on you, but a tumbleweed blows through a place, picking up everything in its path. Bush blew into many people's lives and was blessed with the ability to hold on to those friendships over the years. It was his mother who first taught him understanding and self-awareness. She instilled the virtue of sharing the credit when he won and taking the blame in a loss. Whenever he would tell his mother of his accomplishments in sports, she would reply, "That's great, but how did the team do?" As president, when reviewing his speeches, 41 often crossed out the pronoun "I." Bush understood the relationships he gained over the journey of life were more important than thinking only of himself. His kind and empathetic leadership style attracted—and retained—long-term relationships.

Warming Our Cold Wars

One of the greatest experiences of my life was my selection to the Presidential Leadership Scholars program, to whom I've dedicated this book. Over the last five years, I have joined sixty other scholars from across the country in exploring the leadership lessons from four presidents: George H. W. Bush, George W. Bush, Bill Clinton, and Lyndon Johnson. Being briefed by colleagues in each presidential administration and spending time with the presidents was certainly a once-in-a-lifetime experience. The deep dive into their presidencies will enlighten and impact me for a lifetime. I was also surprised by another transformative aspect of the program—the relationships built with my fellow scholars. Politically and professionally, this program has gathered the most diverse group of people, and I found that I was often polar opposite in my perspectives and beliefs from others. The easy step would have been to position myself with those most like me and offer the friendly smile to the rest. Instead, I chose to pursue friendships with those most unlike me in every way. We had many disagreements, heated discussions, misunderstandings, and revelations, yet we grew deeply committed to working together on what we have in common. This group of strangers quickly transformed into friends, and for many, a new family. Instead of letting the cold war of political and personal differences divide us, we chose to harness our differences as collective strength. Have we all agreed to believe the same things? Nope. But will we let those differences sever our relationships? Not a chance.

In the political arena, President George Bush many times set the example for building empathetic relationships that ended society's "cold wars." He also avoided personal celebrity and maintained the humility that fertilized the rich soil of strong relationships. After the fall of the Berlin Wall and the subsequent collapse of the Soviet Union, President Bush realized that in order to capitalize on the end of the Cold War and nuclear arms race, he needed to embrace both Mikhail Gorbachev and Boris Yeltsin. We can easily forget how high tensions were during the Cold War between the United States and the Soviet Union. The Soviets were our greatest enemies and the animosity between the two countries reached a fever pitch in the second half of the twentieth century. For President Bush to deal with the Soviets as "friends" rather than archenemies, he enabled pathways to peace that previously were not thought realistic. Former Ambassador R. Nicholas Burns, the director of Soviet affairs under President Bush, recounts how the president built relationships with both the outgoing Gorbachev and his main rival, Yeltsin.

> *"He decided he needed to talk to both of them," Burns said, noting that each time he spoke to one, he told the other that he did and what they talked about. "He cultivated two very different Soviet leaders in the autumn of 1991. And it was really quite masterful. It was very impressive, especially in hindsight."*

> *"We all admired him so much, everyone who worked for him. We admired his professionalism, his intellect; he was a listener; he was fair; he was someone with a very strong sense of right and wrong. He had clear integrity when you watched him."*[34]

When the Berlin Wall came down, President Bush faced intense scrutiny and criticism when he offered the very restrained response, "I am very pleased." President Bush refused a victory dance over the Wall, knowing such action would destabilize Gorbachev and threaten the ongoing pathway to peace. It was this restraint from gloating and emotionally charged rhetoric that retained his relationship with Gorbachev and his subsequent ability to negotiate the Strategic Arms Reduction Treaty. The president's long relationship with Gorbachev cultivated the kindness that spared the relationship even if it cost the president public criticism.

In my own life, I learned a lot about empathetic leadership the hard way. As a very young leader who ended up in the role of senior pastor, I often found myself mishandling situations with other people on my team. Too often I was abrupt in my demeanor, without compassion for what might be taking place in their life, and my words were often careless and cutting. It's not that I did not care for them as individuals. I simply was not careful in what I communicated to them.

One day, a seasoned minister on our team pulled me aside. He offered me some unsolicited but much needed advice.

"Brent," he said, "you have two beautiful little girls." (At the time they were about six and four.) "If Berkeley tells Briley her dress is ugly, they are going to get into a little fight. Briley will get her feelings hurt, but she will make Berkeley pay for what she said about her dress. But, Brent, if you tell Briley her dress is ugly, you haven't only hurt her feelings, but you have crushed her spirit." Then he turned this story back to our office. "When you criticize a staff member, you need to be careful what you say and how you say it. You may think your comment is not a big deal when, in fact, you are crushing their spirits. Your words matter, and you need to remember your role as a leader."

Those words stung in a good kind of way. I didn't like to hear it, but I needed it. Actually, I needed those words in my office as well as my main role as a father. And maybe you needed to hear those words as well. My perspective was forever changed by that encounter and now when I talk to people on my team, that image of my kids guides my words, tone, and demeanor.

LEADERS KNOW WHEN TO BE SILENT AND WHEN TO SPEAK

Not everyone has a bold colleague to confront them regarding their lack of empathy. Certainly, very few—if any of us—will ever be in a position of censorship for the U.S. Navy. But we can certainly learn from these examples that

---

words matter

---

when it comes to building empathic relationships. It was the powerful, personal words written on the pages of naval officers' letters to loved ones that transformed President Bush's ability to understand people. It was the words he chose *not* to speak at the fall of the Berlin Wall that strengthened his relationship with Gorbachev and proved his integrity as a colleague. In the words of Winston Churchill, "We are masters of the unsaid word, but slaves of those we let slip out." Bush mastered his words, and used them as a powerful force, even when they were left unspoken.

In the same way, leaders must be diligent about choosing words that strengthen relationships, convey understanding, and build trust. Leaders who master their words wield a weapon that cultivates both empathy and loyalty.

Empathy also requires listening. President Bush did not just read the letters from soldiers, he *heard* what their words represented. He learned to listen to a different story than the ones that previously defined their relationships. President Bush modeled that *listening matters*. Leaders must be relentless, adept listeners—often "hearing" unspoken words. Gorbachev certainly listened to Bush's response to the Berlin Wall during that press conference. Gorbachev did not hear Bush gloat, but he did *hear* the restraint that translated to loyalty and trust in their relationship. Bush, in turn, had orchestrated many opportunities to listen to Gorbachev—even during his vice presidency when he would accompany Gorbachev by car to the airport for his departure from talks with President Reagan. These "car talks" were cited in Gorbachev's memorial to President Bush as critical moments in building their relationship. "The overarching principle of effective listening is to seek first to understand, then to be understood," says Rick Fulwiler, a director at the Harvard School of Public Health, and the former director of health and safety worldwide at Procter and Gamble. Leaders build empathetic relationships by understanding words matter and listening matters.

LEADERS SET RATIONAL BOUNDARIES

Do you have any canaries in your life? That is probably not a question you have ever been asked, yet for many, it may be one of the most important questions in life.

In his book *The Emotionally Healthy Leader*, Peter Scazzero tells about the role of canaries in coal mines. Long before we had advanced, high-tech equipment, coal miners used a simple life hack that literally saved their lives. When mines were being dug deep into the earth, gasses like carbon monoxide were often released and were undetectable to the miners until it was too late. Canaries became the simple solution. Canaries apparently really enjoy life because they sing all day long. Their little lungs were particularly susceptible to gasses like carbon monoxide and when they stopped singing, that was a warning to the miners it was time to get out as quickly as possible. Ignoring those tiny birds could literally mean life or death.

We all need canaries in our lives—someone or something to indicate to us all might not be right in our personal atmosphere. While this is true in many areas of our life, it is certainly true when it comes to a leader's relationships. When we don't have canaries in our lives who have the freedom to speak openly and honestly, we can allow relationships to cloud the ultimate vision. Sometimes close relationships can also negatively impact our ability to make clear decisions.

Ulysses S. Grant needed canaries in his life who could warn him of the danger lurking in his administration. Sadly, the canaries around him during his presidency were not very trustworthy. Later in his life, one man would serve as a friend and advisor. That man was Samuel Clemens, better known as Mark Twain.

Mark Twain once said, "Never allow someone to be your priority while allowing yourself to be their option." President Grant could have benefited from this wit and wisdom years earlier. Following his landslide election, he faced the challenging task of filling cabinet positions and key appointments in his administration. President Grant, however, proved to be a poor judge of character, loyal to a fault, while having a penchant for appointing friends and family over more qualified candidates.

As a result of his inability to set relational boundaries, he allowed undue influence and just plain ignorance to derail his presidency. According to biographer Ron Chernow,

> *The Grants and Dents (his in-laws) showed no scruples about badgering Grant for jobs and he found it hard to avoid the perils of nepotism. The subject of Grant and nepotism remains a puzzle. The practice hurt his standing and detracted from his better cabinet appointments. As Carl Shurz protested, "Grant showed a disposition to give offices to all his relatives and a great number of close personal friends; and in these instances to consult the members of Congress very little. That makes bad blood here and there."*[35]

By his second term, Grant's presidency was peppered with various scandals. In the late 1870s, Grant's secretary of the treasury uncovered a whiskey tax avoidance scheme involving old Civil War friends of Grant. Some of the funds were siphoned to the Republican Party. Grant stated, "Let no guilty man escape if it can be avoided." On further investigation, Grant's personal secretary, Orville Babcock, was implicated. Unable to believe Babcock's guilt, Grant sought to testify on his behalf. Soon thereafter, a newspaper noted the irony of Grant's earlier words and restated his true meaning, "Let no guilty man escape, unless he lives in the palace."[36] It was his inability to set relational boundaries and avoid nepotism that ultimately led to Grant's decision to not run for a third term. In 1875, Grant completely stepped away from involvement in the 1876 election.

President Grant's experience is not an uncommon cautionary tale for leaders across all industries. Few football fans can forget the sad demise of Joe Paterno, head coach of the Penn State Nittany Lions for forty-five years. Lovingly called JoePa, Paterno became the winningest coach in NCAA Division 1 history. Yet, it was his inability to make tough decisions regarding his assistant coach, Jerry Sandusky, that ultimately led to his removal and the dark cloud that now shrouds his legacy.

This tragic story is yet another reminder that

---

leaders must evaluate their relationships and be mindful of personal and professional boundaries.

Many leaders face pressure to hire, promote, and favor friends, family, and people of influence. However, the price can be steep when these relationships take precedence over the position or task at hand. Many people can repeat the words of President Grant's 1876 annual address to Congress: "Mistakes have been made ... and I admit ... [But] failures have been errors of judgment, not of intent." Unfortunately, boundary errors are still errors.

Just as important as setting relational boundaries, leaders should make relational adjustments with decency and integrity. Jim McGrath, spokesman and speechwriter for 41, called President George H. W. Bush "nearly as perfect a man as you can find." According to McGrath, who also worked as deputy press secretary in the Bush White House, "The president always accomplished what he wanted but was able to do it without plowing through people. Decency and accomplishment can go hand in hand." Setting boundaries and maintaining the dignity of all people involved is a difficult dance. Yet, if done well, it serves all parties involved. At one point in Bush's presidency, the NRA sharply criticized law enforcement, calling police officers "thugs." President Bush, a lifetime member of the NRA, did not hesitate to cancel his membership and remind the NRA of the boundaries of decency and dignity that had been transgressed.

Setting relational boundaries as a leader is important but especially true when tough personnel decisions have to be made. Friendships and close relationships can keep leaders from making the best decision for the organizations out of fear of hurting a friend. Situations such as these require wisdom to know what is best for the organization and what is best for the individual. Bold leadership mixed with compassion for the employee is necessary in order to make the right decision. This is why canaries in our lives are so important. They make us aware of the atmosphere around us and can give sage advice for our leadership and our own good.

LEADERS LEVERAGE RELATIONSHIPS

Physicists and financiers are very familiar with leverage. Leverage—in these professions—refers to the utilization of various physical and business tools to greatly increase an outcome. The Greek physicist Archimedes said, "Give me a lever long enough and a fulcrum on which to place it, and I shall move the world." Likewise, many prominent businesses have relied on relational leverage to accomplish very complex mergers and move their world. My father understood this well. He has always instructed me:

> *If you want to see progress in your vision, dreams, or projects, you have to build relationships. The world runs on relationships and if you can't build and maintain strong relationships, you'll never reach your full potential. The way you build relationships is by listening to other people. In the first thirty days of your job, listen. In the next thirty, listen, then do it again for another thirty days. Once you have started listening, you're ready to move forward. But never forget, it's all about relationships.*

My father is not a Greek physicist like Archimedes, but he understands the science of how the rest of the world moves.

President Bush was a master at leveraging relationships to accomplish sweeping vision. Not only did he leverage powerful relationships to build a great domestic team, he utilized his friendships with foreign leaders to solidify the end of the Cold War, strengthen relations with China, and unify what may be history's largest coalition of thirty-nine countries during the Gulf War. His skill at developing and maintaining relations that endured, served him well throughout his presidency and, indeed, his lifetime.

The Iraqi invasion of Kuwait in 1990 opened the door for the president to employ his strength of diplomacy worldwide. Leveraging a meeting with Prime Minister Margaret Thatcher of Great Britain, the president was able to immediately come out swinging with official support from an important ally. He then personally contacted international leaders who would eventually form the coalition to force an Iraqi withdrawal. Drawing from the many relationships he had formed while serving as Ambassador to the United Nations under President Nixon, President Bush did not hesitate to leverage these relationships—underscored by his strong ties with the United Nations—to authorize a U.S.-led coalition. The president was also successful in garnering Congressional support sanctioning the use of military force in Operation Desert Storm. In fact, Mark Updegrove, executive director of the Lyndon B. Johnson Foundation, cites this accomplishment as the ultimate illustration of President Bush's diplomacy prowess.

During that same time, the president was dealing with the fallout from the Tiananmen Square massacre and the delicate trade relations with China. The relationships he had built during his two-year appointment under President Ford as unofficial U.S. envoy to China in 1974 shaped his diplomacy years later. He was sharply criticized by Congress for not imposing harsher sanctions upon China as punishment for their violent reaction to the protestors in Tiananmen Square. Yet, due to his restraint and his understanding of China's leaders, the president was able to maintain the delicate relations and repair some of the damage done to U.S.-Sino affairs.

Similarly, President Bush faced a challenge after the Berlin Wall during the debates about the reunification of Germany. Bush—who usually favored gradual, measured change—was met with events in 1989 moved along at such a rapid pace that President Bush's natural inclination toward gradual change was severely challenged. Discussions progressed quickly and several options were outlined and discussed by the United States, France, Britain, and the Soviet Union operating under postwar agreements. Not only did they ultimately agree on a reunification strategy, but President Bush helped negotiate a compromise so that the newly united Germany would be a member of NATO.

Be a Tumbleweed

The ability of President Bush to develop and maintain relationships over his lifetime clearly served him well as he leveraged relationships towards greater goals. His past experiences and the friendships he formed were key factors in his foreign policy advances. Conversely, Grant's inability to move beyond his close circle of friends and family—and those he considered natural confidantes—hampered his abilities at diplomacy.

Effective leaders must learn to be a "tumbleweed," building relationships that "stick." Leaders must also take great care in developing and nurturing sincere relationships. While maintaining an extensive contact list is valuable, the individuals listed are the ones who hold the real value. In an era of garnering contacts with both business and personal social media tools, it is often difficult to distinguish between true relationships and "the six people that lead to Kevin Bacon."

Leverage does not mean using relationships as commodities.

Rather, you must remember that people matter, brands and ideas matter, and good boundaries matter. But ultimately, it's about people. Keeping these ideas in mind sets the framework for successful coordinated effort.

Saved by the Pen Pal

President Bush's *Catch Me If You Can* lifetime approach to building relationships far outdistanced the presidential leadership skills of Ulysses Grant. Maybe you can identify with Grant, and to date, have not focused on relationship-building skills and networking with others who advance your greater goals. Take heart. It was one simple relationship that resurrected Grant's goal of providing for his family and leaving a strong legacy behind.

It was Mark Twain who convinced Grant to write his memoirs after he lost his fortune in the investment scandal at his son's firm and Mark Twain who offered him a lucrative publishing contract and provided for his needs while he wrote. It was his relationship with Mark Twain that sparked his interest in writing and gave him the fortitude and perseverance to write, literally finishing his memoirs days before his death. Twain gave Grant one final opportunity to provide for his family and leave the legacy he desired. Seek the Mark Twain in your life! Nurture that relationship, set boundaries and leverage the friendship towards visionary collaboration. You have to start somewhere, so start with the power of one. Like Grant, you may discover new skills, new motivation and a greater vision.

Somewhere in the Philippines there is a boy named Timothy, who unbeknownst to him, was a pen pal with the former President of the United States. "G. Walker" never met the young boy to whom he wrote faithfully until his death. This relationship was never leveraged to accomplish anything, other than confirm to those closest to him that the president was truly a man of dignity and integrity. Yet, leaders never cease to build relationships because it impacts future leaders, future diplomatic efforts, future generations. And maybe, thanks to the legacy of President Bush, boys like Timothy and leaders in generations to come—all over the world—will believe, "The only thing that really matters in life are your relationships to other people.

Chapter 7

Abraham Lincoln & Richard M. Nixon

Leaders Forgive

"Everybody has a little bit of Watergate in him."
–Reverend Billy Graham

*"The strength of this country isn't in buildings of brick and steel. It's
in the hearts of those who have sworn to fight for its freedom."*
–Captain America

On April 9, 1865, General Robert E. Lee sat at attention in
the home of Wilmer McLean, a citizen of Appomattox Court
House. Lee's stalwart six-foot frame filled the sitting room
window, casting an immovable shadow over the parlor. His gray Confederate uniform was buttoned to the neck under his thick gray beard.

Nearing his sixtieth birthday, he maintained the youthful posture of a soldier—his spurs securely fitted around his boots and a polished sword resting by his side. His face was expressionless, yet his eyes held the secrets of the bloody battlefields where he had stepped over thousands of soldiers a third his age.

General Ulysses S. Grant quietly stepped into the room and took a seat at the marble table in the center. His shoulders were slightly stooped under a dark flannel shirt, unbuttoned to mid- chest. His five foot eight frame lowered to the table, where he rubbed his chestnut beard. Wearing no spurs and wielding no weapon, the forty-three-year-old sat in casual contrast to the man in gray.

Two and a half hours later, the surrender was official. General Lee had asked General Grant to record the terms in an official document. General Grant's pen did not stop until the terms of surrender were complete. As Grant paused at the end of the agreement, he glanced thoughtfully at General Lee and added, "This will not embrace the sidearms of the officers, nor their private horses or baggage."

General Lee rose and shook hands to seal the surrender. Grant commented later that it would have been an unnecessary act of humiliation to confiscate the Confederate Army's swords, personal effects, and horses. Grant then instructed his officers to salute as Lee silently mounted his horse to face his defeated Confederate Army.

Surely General Grant bore the impact of the words spoken by his commander in chief, who just a month earlier had delivered his second inaugural address to a great crowd at the Capitol. On March 4, 1865, President Lincoln's words set the table that ended the Civil War: "With malice toward none, with charity for all, with firmness in the right as God gives us to see the right, let us strive on to finish the work we are in, to bind up the nation's wounds, to care for him who shall have borne the battle and for his widow and his orphan, to do all which may achieve and cherish a just and lasting peace among ourselves and with all nations."

Known for his magnanimity and grace, the president's ardent and humble appeal to a nation—just weeks before his assassination—proved that he was much more than "Honest Abe." He was a leader unafraid to conquer humanity's greatest war—the battle over forgiveness and grace towards fellow man.

President Abraham Lincoln won his first term of office in 1860. One century later, after losing his first attempt at the presidency to John F. Kennedy, Nixon clawed through the ranks and was elected to his first term in office in 1968. His meteoric rise to power, and his early domestic and international accomplishments, secured a landslide victory for his second term in 1972. Like Lincoln, he was credited with the official ending of a controversial and bloody war in Vietnam when he signed the Paris Peace Accords a year later. Yet, in the end, it was his inability to adopt the forgiveness, grace, and magnanimity modeled by Lincoln that tarnished his legacy and made him the only president to resign his post. Like General Grant, incoming President Ford saluted Nixon with a full pardon for his transgressions. But unlike General Lee, Nixon eschewed the honor and rode away embittered and vengeful. His eyes flashing, he did not refrain his speech towards his enemies but let his mouth tell his version of the story—a trait which had earned him the nickname "Tricky Dick." In stark contrast, Lincoln's former political rival and newly appointed secretary of state, William Seward, once commented that Lincoln's "magnanimity is almost superhuman."

Had President Lincoln and President Nixon met in the Marvel Universe as superhero characters, they would at first glance appear to favor Captain America: both suffering devastating personal losses with the death of Nixon's brothers and Lincoln's mother and sons; both hearty debaters—Lincoln with Douglas and Nixon with Kennedy; both serving in the military and enjoying a political career in the Republican Party; both wartime presidents settling unpopular and devastating wars, and both theater lovers. But where Lincoln would continue to grow into the heart and soul of Captain America, Nixon's interpersonal dealings and dishonest choices would eventually gravitate to the grand theater of antihero, *Ghost Rider*, and his *Spirit of Vengeance*. Even in the superhero universe, it is those who act out of magnanimity that eventually save the day—and themselves.

To explore the leadership of Lincoln and Nixon is to view both an inspirational epic and a cautionary tale about the supernatural battle to forgive, show grace, and honor others above yourself. Make no mistake, this is a bloodier battlefield than the Civil War and the Vietnam Conflict combined. Leaders who take up their shield like Captain America, however, will marvel at the greatest victory of them all—the victory over their own will.

TO ERR IS HUMAN, TO FORGIVE, INFREQUENT—LEADERS FORGIVE

As a pastor, one of the most difficult situations I encounter is when those seeking counsel either refuse to apologize, or offer forgiveness. The damage that is incurred by everyone in the room is incalculable. Yet, I also realize, some hurts are so deep that this task can seem almost impossible. Usually, when someone first approaches an apology, there is a "but" in the sentence: "I'm really sorry, *but* if you wouldn't have done …" Or many times, those offering forgiveness take the opportunity to rub someone's nose into what has occurred one last time. Victimhood and vengeance are always lurking at the doors of contrition and mercy. Failing to battle through these threats not only destroys the relationship, it also destroys the individuals who are mastered by them. Great leaders have wrestled through the root causes of vengeance and victimhood, and replaced them with the gift of forgiveness. And for those who have mastered that battle, they realize that the gift is actually theirs.

Leaders Can't Carry Grudges and Forgiveness at the Same Time

I had a friend whose daughter lived in a small apartment in New York City with her seventy-pound Doberman. Sadly, the dog took ill and passed away. When she called the veterinarian, they asked that she bring the dog to their office so that they could take care of the dog's remains. She didn't own a car and was perplexed about how to transport her dog, when she spied a large roller suitcase in her closet. She wrapped the dog in garbage bags, successfully loaded the dog's body into the suitcase, and rolled the large bag towards the subway.

Unfortunately, when she reached the subway entrance, the suitcase was so large it got stuck as she attempted to go through the turnstile. She was on the inside pulling the bag to no avail. A man walked up behind the bag and asked her to let go, so he could push the bag for her. She gratefully accepted his offer and stared in shock as he grabbed the bag and took off for the street. By the weight of the bag, the thief must have thought he had just hit a goldmine. One can only imagine his expression when he finally unzipped the suitcase and beheld his ill-gotten loot.

In the same way, many people carry around baggage in their lives that are filled with "death." Grudges, anger, resentment, and disappointments fill suitcases many people drag around for years. The deadly content of those bags pulls people down and hold them back from experiencing the joys of life. Typically, it makes the person constantly frustrated, often angry, and difficult to be around. Unless addressed, people find it can destroy their lives. Leaders need to spend the time to unpack their grudges and offload the weight of bitterness, vengeance, and scorn. If they refuse to learn alternatives like mercy, kindness, and compassion, their baggage will eventually start to stink and infect those around them.

In the hours before Richard Nixon left office, he called aids, friends, and family to the West Wing of the White House. During a meandering speech, he spoke of grievances past and present, including how his mother was mistreated and his father struggled with poverty. As he closed his presentation, he raised his hand to indicate that he was getting to the point, "Always remember that others will hate you, but those who hate you will not win, unless you hate them and then you destroy yourself." According to Bob Woodward, the *Washington Post* reporter who exposed the Watergate scandal, Nixon's hatred was the poison that destroyed his own personal life as well as his presidency.

There is usually a moment of clarity, when we have a chance to choose our path. Natural instinct leads towards revenge and it is often an act of will to fight for forgiveness. For Nixon, that moment came and went when he decided to seek vengeance on whistleblower Daniel Ellsberg. With the stress of Vietnam protests and public indignation every time a flag-draped body was flown home, Nixon became more and more paranoid, often turning to vitriol and vices. Daniel Ellsberg had been a defense analyst in the Pentagon with classified knowledge of the Vietnam War. During the Nixon administration, he was working at the Rand Corporation as part of a team that developed the *Pentagon Papers*—a classified report confirming government deceit when communicating with the American people regarding the war.

Ellsberg copied the report and went to the *New York Times,* who decided to take their legal chances and publish the classified documents in a series on its front page. On Sunday, June 13, 1971, the first article appeared: "Vietnam Archive: Pentagon Study Traces Three Decades of Growing US Involvement." That marker, along with his own paranoia, eventually led Nixon to believe there was a great leftist conspiracy against the Office of the President, and he vowed to defend himself and his office at all costs—even at the cost of breaking the law. When the Supreme Court ruled that the *Times* could continue publishing the papers, Nixon took vengeance into his own hands, orchestrating what eventually became known as the Watergate scandal. According to Woodward, whose *Wash-*

ington Post had also obtained the same information from Ellsberg, Nixon often used the presidency as an office of personal revenge—utilizing agencies like the FBI and the U.S. Treasury to harass enemies. Thanks to a revelation that Nixon had secretly installed a sophisticated recording system, his surrender of the tapes confirmed his crimes and ultimately led to his resignation.

Nixon's moment of clarity came far too late, as a rambling speech on his way out of office. At least he had the sentience to acknowledge that his own hatred was the currency that paid for his resignation. The suffering he created for himself and his family was paid out over a lifetime. According to former adviser Leonard Garment, "It was a 'paradox.' When wounded, Nixon was both strengthened—in that he drew renewed confidence from surviving—and weakened, in that he just could not forgive, or forget, or bring a halt to his self-destructive gnashing."[37]

Author and architect of the personal growth industry and founder of *The Successful Mind Podcast*, David Neagle, learned about forgiveness the hard way. Swindled out of five million dollars, he was at a crossroads: pursue legal action to the tune of $250,000 and years of litigation, or forgive and start to rebuild his business. He chose to step on the positive path of rebuilding rather than the road to legal restitution. As a result, he was able to get back on his feet quickly and learned valuable lessons through the process. He lists his four keys to forgiveness and healing as:

- Accepting responsibility for his role
- Creating a plan
- Being thankful
- Letting go of anger.

In his words, he realized "you cannot hold onto resentment and move forward at the same time."[38] He credits this valuable lesson to tremendous growth in his own life and career.

Life on the Monkey Bars

Once leaders have "unpacked their suitcase," particularly baggage from the past, they then must put the suitcase away, refusing to carry it again. I have referred to this step as "Life on the Monkey Bars." Author C. S. Lewis said:

"Getting over a painful experience is much like crossing monkey bars—let go to move forward."

We all remember the monkey bars from our childhood days on the playground. The key to the apparatus is strength, inertia, and one critical point—you must let go of the bar behind you to move ahead to the one in front of you. You truly cannot move forward without loosening your grip and letting go of the previous rung.

Leaders must look within themselves to examine if they need to release grudges in order to bring forgiveness within reach. In the same way, they should be mindful of management and staff that may need assistance doing the same. The art of leadership is prioritizing people over organizations. Your will find that it is a privilege to help others find ways to let go of the past and reach for the future.

The Write Path to Forgiveness

One effective, practical tool to assist in the process of forgiveness can be applied by all—writing it out. Abraham Lincoln had the marvelous ability to forgive, and he utilized his gift of writing in the process. The second inaugural address given in the final days of the Civil War shares a broad view of the plan for national healing and a glimpse into Lincoln's leadership commitment to forgiveness and grace. To appreciate why his address is so remarkable requires understanding the hell Lincoln had been through leading up to the speech.

Immediately upon his election, South Carolina took steps to secede from the Union, the first in a long line of states to do so. Lincoln had been called upon to send men and boys to their deaths, one of the highest and most difficult responsibilities of the commander in chief. He had been the target of numerous assassination plots, berated by some of his own generals, maligned in the press, and weighed down under the constant pressures in his position as president.

In order to move towards forgiveness, he dealt with the many hurtful comments that were hurled at him by writing what he called "hot letters" of response to his critics. He unleashed his pen, often chastising his opponents for their ignorance, stupidity, and hatefulness. Once his anger was spent, he placed the letters in a drawer, never to be delivered. After this personal process of acknowledging the emotions of injustice, he was able to speak healing words to the nation (and the Confederacy). The discipline of writing advanced both personal and corporate healing and allowed him to express the injustice in a safe, productive manner. He was then able to move towards forgiveness.

When considering forgiveness there are four basic attitudes that arise:

1. **I Won't:** This attitude says I have been hurt but it does not stop at the offense. The pain becomes a lifelong obsession and bitterness will dominate that person's life. The refusal to deal with the issue of forgiveness is poison to the soul.

2. **I Can't:** Some people feel the hurt that has happened in their life is too much. They feel they could never forgive the person who has caused them pain. Believing that forgiveness would let the offender off the hook, they refuse to even consider forgiveness. Usually "I Can't" is just a nicer way of saying "I Won't."

3. **I Don't Want To:** This response is probably the most honest. It is a tacit admission that the individual would rather hold onto the hurt than forgive. Often, they understand the ramifications of

holding on to the pain, but it has almost become addictive and they cannot imagine life any other way.

4. **I Am Willing:** This is the hardest response and is usually followed by the phrase "Lord, help me." To say that you are willing to forgive will require a great heart and tremendous courage. Choosing to forgive is the path less traveled, but it is the path to healing and hope.

Once you are *willing*, unpack your suitcase, put it away, record the injustice, and find a safe place to be honest without harming others. You will then free your grip from the previous monkey bar. In the words of Max Lucado, "Forgiveness is unlocking the door to set someone free and realizing you were the prisoner!"

CAPTAIN MAGNANIMITY—LEADERS MUST BE BIGGER THAN THEMSELVES

What was it about Abraham Lincoln that allowed him to respond, by word and deed, "with malice toward none, with charity for all"? I think it can best be described in one little-used word: magnanimity. It is defined as "generous in forgiving an insult or injury, free from petty resentfulness or vindictiveness." It is derived from the Latin root *magna*—meaning great—and *animus*—meaning mind. To be magnanimous is to be greater in your mind and in your life—essentially, greatness of the soul. Aristotle called it "the crowning virtue." I like to call it "being bigger than yourself." Abraham Lincoln was the essence of magnanimity seen clearly in his ability to forgive, his humility in office, and his grace towards others. These are the ingredients of a mind set on being bigger than itself.

Leaders Put the Best People in the Best Places

One of the greatest examples of Lincoln's ability to be "bigger than himself" is told by Doris Kearns Goodwin in her magnificent biography, *Team of Rivals: The Political Genius of Abraham Lincoln*. The story involves an encounter with Edwin Stanton years before Lincoln became president. Lincoln was assigned to handle a legal case with Stanton who, at the time, knew very little about the young country lawyer. Lincoln painstakingly prepared a detailed brief on the case for his "partner," but Stanton refused to even read it, tossing it into the trash. Stanton referred to Lincoln as that "long-armed ape" and refused to treat him as an equal. Yet years later, when the now President Lincoln needed to replace his Secretary of War, he chose Stanton, the man who had previously maligned and hurt him so badly. When questioned why he would choose Stanton for this position after having been mistreated by him, Lincoln replied that he believed he was the best man for the job. The qualities that had made Edwin Stanton hot-headed and caused him to treat Lincoln badly would be the same qualities needed to bolster his determination to succeed as secretary of war. Lincoln did not hold a grudge, but instead chose to forgive and honor the individual—irrespective of Stanton's posture towards him. In Lincoln's words, "I destroy my enemies when I make them my friends."

Lincoln made a habit of selecting the best individual for the job, despite past differences. In fact, three men chosen for his cabinet—William H. Seward, Salmon P. Chase, and Edward Bates—had been his opponents for the Republican nomination in 1860. William Seward—Lincoln's chief rival—became one of his main advisors, serving as secretary of state. Known for his decision to purchase Alaska, according to Lincoln, Seward was a man "without gall." Seward worked very closely with the president. He said of Lincoln in a private letter to his wife "his magnanimity is almost superhuman."

Those cabinet members who were rivals had a very low view of the president upon their appointments. However, after working with him daily, they grew to revere and honor the president's unquestionable character.

Warren Buffet, CEO of Berkshire Hathaway and a prolific investor, looks for three character traits in potential employees: integrity, intelligence, and energy.[39] He has famously quipped: "If you don't have the first, the other two will kill you. If you hire somebody without integrity, you really want them to be dumb and lazy." Add magnanimity and you will get all three and more. Leaders must both possess integrity and demand that in others. This magnificent quality will surround them with a force field of superheroes—individuals who are "bigger than themselves."

Leaders Master Pride

In any good superhero movie or comic book, there is an antihero. Usually a good guy gone rogue, these antiheros are no longer fueled by good "serum," but instead, their superpowers feed off of revenge, often disguised as justice. In the Marvel Universe, Robbie Reys was a young Los Angeles car mechanic who was murdered and then brought back to life by a former motorcycle stuntman named Johnnie Blaze. Blaze had made a pact with a demon to save his beloved father figure and, as a result, was bound with the spirit of vengeance which he passed on to Reys. Together they became part of the ghost riders, using their superpowers to seek vengeance on perpetrators through violence at night.[40]

While you may be unfamiliar with the superhero world, it is not much different than our reality in some respects. Vengeance is a universal, innate reaction for all of humanity, usually born out of terrible injustice. Antiheros, like the ghost riders, were known for revenge— tormenting criminals and other wrongdoers by taking matters into their own hands. They justify their violence because it is directed towards evil. The problem is that when unchecked, vengeance—like fuel to a flame—becomes an inferno that devours everyone when perspective is lost.

The root cause of vengeance is pride—the mistaken belief that you can right all wrongs in your own way.

As Nixon found, this pride-fueled vengeance was the first step to justifying law-breaking during Watergate. He lost perspective and failed to master the pride that ruled his life.

Keeps No Record of Wrongs

As revealed during the Watergate scandal, President Nixon kept an official enemies list under the direction of Special Counsel Charles Colson, also known as his "hatchet man." The document described "how we can use the available federal machinery to screw our political enemies."[41] This secret agenda empowered President Nixon to misuse federal agencies, such as the Internal Revenue Service, as "personal weapons" to attack his enemies. Driven by vengeance and pride, he justified using his office—much like in the Ellsberg instance—to abuse his power. He had not mastered his pride; he was mastered by it. Ultimately, this list became yet another piece of incriminating evidence in Article II of his impeachment charges.

> He has, acting personally and through his subordinates and agents, endeavored to obtain from the Internal Revenue Service, in violation of the constitutional rights of citizens, confidential information contained in the income tax returns for purposes not authorized by law, and to cause, in violation of the constitutional rights of citizens, income tax audits or other income tax investigations to be initiated or conducted in a discriminatory manner.[42]

Truly, when it came to abuse of power, Nixon was an antihero in disguise. It is better to be the villain than the antihero. At least villains are honest and know who they are. The antihero is mastered by pride, which in turn fuels the deceit that justifies wrongdoing. Many leaders have been entangled in the web of vengeance and retribution, and we have all witnessed organizations fall apart with antiheroes at the helm. Be the superhero. Master your pride and don't make a deal with vengeance.

You Were Right and I Was Wrong

The road to magnanimity is no easy journey. Many forget that President Lincoln did not originally plan to free the slaves. At one point, his idea was to send them back to Liberia. In addition, according to the Miller Center, for Lincoln "it made no sense to lose the nation and yet preserve the Constitution."[43] Therefore, he was accused of transgressing constitutional provisions by expanding the army and navy, spending $2 million without congressional approval, suspending the writ of habeas corpus, and closing post offices to intercept treasonous correspondence. Yet, Lincoln had the humility—and patience with himself—to be correctable.

Following the capture of Vicksburg on July 4, 1863, President Lincoln wrote a letter to his general, Ulysses S. Grant. In the letter, he acknowledged that though they have never met face-to-face, he wanted to commend him for his service to the country. Lincoln first expressed his agreement with certain strategies enacted by Grant, and then admitted there was one tactic Grant made in which the president had disagreed.

> *When you got below, and took Port-Gibson, Grand Gulf, and vicinity, I thought you should go down the river and join Gen. Banks; and when you turned Northward East of the Big Black, I feared it was a mistake. I now wish to make the personal acknowledgment that you were right, and I was wrong. Yours very truly, A. Lincoln*[44]

To hear a President sincerely admit he was mistaken is rare. Our culture often interprets acknowledgement of failure as weakness. However, like forgiveness, contrition takes a remarkable amount of strength—and patience. Leaders often impose a standard of perfectionism as the measure of self-evaluation. Their own standards often breed their impatience with themselves, and others.

Do not lose sight of the reality that leadership is not immune to errors. Willingness to admit you were wrong will not diminish your reputation in the eyes of your followers, but actually increase their esteem for your character. Like the cabinet members appointed by President Lincoln, those you lead will observe and respect your contrition as a sign of integrity. Exercising patience with yourself and others paves the highway on the road to forgiveness and grace.

Put on Your Cape

An adolescent Teddy Roosevelt peeked out the window of his uncle's apartment to watch the procession behind the coffin of his hero, President Abraham Lincoln. This young boy shared the shock of the nation following the first presidential assassination in American history. No one could comprehend that the legacy of the man who settled the states rights' controversy, preserved the republic, and ended slavery was over. Thankfully, his legacy was not over. In fact, it is forever woven into the fabric of our nation.

The day Richard Nixon left office, incoming president Gerald Ford solemnly waved, calling it "one of the very saddest incidents I have ever witnessed." The man who hated quitters, became known as the first president in American history to quit. The legacy of this president, who just two years earlier won his second election by carrying forty-nine of the fifty states, was over.

After his resignation, Nixon granted a television interview and admitted: "I let down my friends. I let down the country. I let down our system of government ... Yup, I let the American people down, and I have to carry that burden with me for the rest of my life."

When he left office, President Lincoln had surrendered his burdens and was carried away on his legacy of magnanimity. President Nixon packed his own burdens out of the White House and was given more time on earth to clean out his suitcase. At Nixon's funeral, President Clinton—one of the five living presidents to attend—said, "May the day of judging President Nixon on anything less than his entire life and career come to a close." Like General Grant saluting General Lee, forgiveness and grace finally put Nixon's suitcase away for good and he carried that burden no more.

Forgiveness is the superpower of every leader's endgame. It cleans out the Watergate inside us all. Put on your cape and go be a superhero to someone today.

Chapter 8

Lyndon B. Johnson & James Madison

Leaders Persuade

*"It takes time to persuade men to do
even what is for their own good."*
–Thomas Jefferson

*"I don't play small. You have to go out and play with what you
have. I admit I used to want to be tall. But I made it in high
school, college, and now the pros. So it doesn't matter."*
–Spud Webb

"T he brakes don't work! We're going in! We're going under!"
John Gardner, secretary for health, education, and welfare
under President Lyndon B. Johnson, held on for dear life

as the car driven by the president careened down a hill towards a lake on LBJ's Texas ranch. The president pumped the brakes and fought to control the steering wheel while the passengers screamed and braced themselves to hit water at full speed. As the front end collided with the murky lake, Gardner heard the president roar with laughter while the car began to float and sputter forward. The president had been driving his *amphicar*—a German-made, civilian amphibious passenger automobile, mass-produced from 1961-1968. LBJ embraced modern contraptions and was no stranger to a good prank. To combine the two was endemic to his persuasive personality. These antics helped shape Gardner's later perspective that the president's life had become "a series of great opportunities disguised as insoluble problems." Under the tenure of the thirty-sixth president, Gardner—the only Republican member of LBJ's cabinet—would eventually be persuaded to launch Medicare, influence campaign finance reform, and expand the Elementary and Secondary Education Act during LBJ's Great Society initiative. Like so many others, he encountered the "Johnson Treatment" on more occasions than this. Often, when it appeared the brakes were not working in the Oval Office, it was just the president keeping everything afloat.

A League of Their Own—Players Persuasion Union

The great philosopher Aristotle recorded his thoughts on persuasion in his classic work *Rhetoric*. "We believe good men more fully and more readily than others: this is true generally whatever the question is, and absolutely true where exact certainty is impossible and opinions are divided."

This was absolutely true of two presidents—James Madison and Lyndon Baines Johnson—in the late 1700s and 1960s respectively—especially in the arena of civil rights. Madison established the foundation of our government and the Bill of Rights in the 1700s—and two centuries later, LBJ advanced civil rights more than any other president before him in the 1960s. These good men shaped our nation and utilized the power of persuasion when *exact certainty was impossible and opinions were divided.*

The visual pairing of Presidents Lyndon Johnson and James Madison is like selecting seven foot six post Yao Ming and five foot seven point guard Spud Webb for a one-on-one presidential fantasy league. LBJ, a towering Texan at six foot four was known as an indomitable force. Although he was "big as the state that produced him," on a basketball court he would have preferred to play point guard. A fierce competitor, he liked to control the ball and improvise all of his own, self-styled plays. No stranger to a few technical fouls, he surely would have tangled with the refs from time to time, racking up a Dennis Rodman reputation. Once called "Twenty of the Most Interesting People I Have Ever Met," he would be able to play any position and view himself as the entirety of the team.

Madison, at five foot four, however, would have gladly ridden the bench and waited to be called into the game when absolutely strategically necessary. In the meantime, he would have memorized the playbook and ordered hundreds of treatises on the sport to make sure the game was being played with appropriate awards, boundaries, and penalties. He would also interview fellow players and analyze if the there was a need for a player's union. Once called into the game, he would patiently watch the floor to wait for his opening to run one perfect play.

Madison was the consummate "sixth man" on any team—soft-spoken, methodical, and content with his influence behind the scenes. According to biographer Lynne Cheney, he is remembered "less as a bold thinker and superb politician than as a shy and sickly scholar, someone hardly suited for the demands of daily life, much less the rough-and-tumble world of politicking."[45] LBJ, on the other hand, was always a starter—confident, intuitive, quick-thinking—always dominating the game. He was vague on his reading habits and philosophical mooring yet made up for it by monopolizing conversation. Madison was quiet, contemplative, and deliberate—and once ordered 200 books on philosophy and political systems from Europe to help him shape the Federalist Papers. LBJ could read people like a book and used his physical prowess to lean into those he wanted to persuade. Both men led the nation through times of peril. With the backdrop of the War of 1812 for Madison, and the Vietnam War for LBJ, they similarly sought to convince a very divided nation to improve our federal government by ending conflict and instilling lasting civil rights protections to all people. In other words, #4 and #36 were very different players, but both competed with the purpose of improving the game. Their legacies—both in and out of office—illustrate how utilizing personal stories, taking full advantage of modern communication tools, and committing to a greater purpose are effective tools of persuasion to effect great change.

STORYTELLING IS NOT JUST FOR DISNEY— LEADERS UTILIZE PERSONAL STORIES

Bob Iger, former CEO of Disney, once summed up the purpose and vision of Disney in one simple statement: "We are in the business of storytelling." In his book, *The Ride of a Lifetime: Lessons Learned from 15 Years as CEO of the Walt Disney Company*, Iger details his very personal "rags to riches" story and engages the reader not only in his person, but in the foundation of his leadership vision for Disney. In his words, "Tell a story, and then leverage that story across multiple lines of business and territories."[46] For employees of Disney—and those who love the universal rags to riches plot his story tells—people are emotionally invested in the stories of Iger's past and are persuaded to embrace his vision and purpose for the company.

Similarly, in both the 1700s and the 1960s, the personal stories that shaped both presidents had a dramatic effect on their abilities to persuade the country to support the creation of the Bill of Rights under Madison and legislation, including the Civil Rights Act, under LBJ.

James Madison was the oldest of ten children and a product of British rule. His early years were shaped by the oppression of growing up under the crown and the responsibilities of an oldest child. While most colonists loved their home country and respected the authority of the crown, they resented some of the more nefarious parts of the monarchy. In fact, the Bill of Rights is a direct response, in many ways, to the restrictions placed on everyday citizens. Madison and other Founding Fathers had witnessed the oppressive violation of privacy and personal rights in many aspects of the colonist's lives. In one example, the British government did not have military bases set up across North America and as a result, they would require homeowners—if asked or told—to house soldiers in their homes, barns, or inns. This literally meant that a knock at the door could lead to two or more men sleeping in a colonist's home as uninvited guests. The deep anger of Madison and the other Founding Fathers would ultimately lead to the Third Amendment to the Constitution, which prohibits the quartering of soldiers without homeowner consent.

LBJ was a product of a small Texas town. Greatly influenced by his refined, educated mother and his straight-talking business-minded father, he was exposed to an array of philosophical, political, and business ideas. Like Madison, he was no stranger to oppressive violations of personal rights either. Early in his career, LBJ served as a teacher at a Mexican-American school near the border in Cotulla, Texas. It was there that he encountered firsthand the plight of these marginalized school children. He witnessed the abject hatred, bigotry, and poverty that shaped their lives and the challenges that posed to their education and basic civil liberties. According to CEO of the Lyndon Baines Johnson Foundation,

Mark Updegrove, LBJ made it his purpose to instill hope and ambition in these children—even telling them that they could be president one day.[47] When LBJ served both in the Senate and as president, these stories told through the eyes of the children were used to persuade politicians and the public to pass the Civil Rights Act of 1964.

Modern stories—like the inequality at the Cotulla schools—were often used by LBJ to emotionally persuade lawmakers into action. The Civil Rights Act followed the assassination of President Kennedy; the Voting Rights Act passed following "Bloody Sunday"; and the Fair Housing Act passed following the assassination of Martin Luther King. There was no story that LBJ was unwilling to tell in order to persuade others to action. He was the master at leveraging stories over multiple lines of business and territories to reach a higher goal. In the same way, leaders have to be adept at storytelling to emotionally motivate others. One of the most powerful ways to employ storytelling is to use personal stories and anecdotes that resonate universally with the human experience.

Be Your Own Screenwriter

Leaders must be willing to utilize their past and present circumstances in a very personal way as one of the most effective tools of persuasion. It has often been said that "facts tell, stories sell." You do not have to be the CEO of Disney to tell a compelling story. As a pastor, I was once told that I should see at least one hundred illustrations/stories a day if I would just look around. In fact, the Bible says of Jesus, "He did not say anything to them without using a story."

I have often retold a personal story that has resonated with many over the years. Years ago, on a cold winter day, my wife and I found ourselves outside the set of Good Morning America in New York City. As we watched the anchors interview their well-known guests, we shivered in the cold, marveling at how warm and toasty everyone inside looked. Finally, as the show ended, Diane Sawyer stepped outside and spoke to us. I asked her for a picture with my wife, and immediately she wrapped her warm arms around Allison and smiled for the camera. That story was one I was able to tell over and over again because it demonstrated the importance of people being willing to go beyond their comfort zone to wrap arms around those in need. Not only did Diane Sawyer connect with my wife, but that story has connected with countless others.

In his modern fable, *Saturday Morning Tea: The Power of Story to Change Everything*, businessman, author, and speaker Tony Bridwell writes, "We are hardwired for story. When people are told the right story, we can change the way they think and feel, which energizes their engagement ..."[48]

Whether just relaying mundane acts such as a drive to work, a business story from the boardroom, or the heart-wrenching sickness of a loved one or friend, a story immediately engages the audience and lights the fires of action. In a *Forbes* article entitled "Leadership Is All About Emotional Persuasion," communication theorist Nick Morgan writes:

> *The communicating a leader does is all, essentially, persuasion. That's what leaders do ... Persuasion means changing someone's mind. If the mind isn't changed, the person hasn't been persuaded. It's that simple. So a leader's job is to change minds, to push followers to make new decisions. Here's the surprising thing: decision-making is fundamentally emotional. Recent brain research shows that if you incapacitate the part of the brain concerned with emotions, through a stroke or other brain trauma, people can't make decisions.*

Both Madison and LBJ desperately needed people to make critical decisions. In the aftermath of the Constitutional Convention, as the dissention of the anti-Federalists heightened in the public square, it was the stories told by Madison in the Federalist Papers that moved emotions and actions to ratify the Constitution and create a Bill of Rights. Similarly, during some of the most prolific assassinations in our country's history, LBJ used those stories—undergirded by the story that shaped his life—to move the emotions of the people into transformative, enduring legislation.

Two Ears and One Mouth

Just as critical as the stories chosen, leaders must first listen in order to tell an effective story. The discipline of listening before talking has always been a struggle. That is probably why it is often said that we were given two ears and one mouth. If you want the people you lead to hear your story, you must first listen to better understand the stories that they are inclined to hear. I have found the most efficient way to understand people is to let them talk.

When you encourage people to tell you a bit of their story, you find out insights about them they often would never tell.

With my students I teach in my history classes, on the first day while taking roll, I ask these two questions:

Do you love history or hate history? I let them know the answer will not impact their grade.

Second, if you could hang out with anyone in world history, who would it be?

In a matter of moments I learn a lot about students who enjoy music, play sports, are psychology majors (they always say Hitler), or want to be in public life. As their teacher, the more I listen, the more I learn about my students. What is true in the classroom works even better in the office. Leaders listen.

LBJ was a master listener. According to Larry Temple, "LBJ read people like a book and knew how to play on their ego to get what he needed and wanted." Similarly, Mark Updegrove stated that the real secret to LBJ's power of persuasion was his ability to read the human psyche. He took a keen interest in people and heard their stories before presenting his. He even trained his staff to support his natural interest in people and record detailed notes about the children, habits, and interests of the people he encountered.

Critical to achieving his ambitions, LBJ was able to formulate relationships by listening and remembering the stories that moved his audience. Once, when encouraged by the Senate to quote a passage from Socrates to his fellow Texans in order to motivate their support, LBJ answered, "Socrates? Socrates! I'm going home to Texas and you have me quoting Socrates? So, keep the quote, but start with 'My daddy used to say …'" LBJ knew his audience, and he knew what his audience needed to hear and how they needed to hear it.

Most people would probably find it ironic that the "Father of the Bill of Rights" never wanted to be its dad. Madison, also known as the "Father of the Constitution," believed the original document was so strong and flexible that a bill of rights was not necessary. "If an enumeration be made of our rights, will it not be implied, that every thing omitted [from the list] is given to the general government."[49] Madison originally believed a bill of rights to be unnecessary.

His critics (and friends) disagreed. So Madison—embroiled in the debates following the Constitutional Convention—lent a listening ear to the opposition posed by the anti-Federalists. The great politician, orator, and opponent of the new Constitution, Patrick Henry, cried out, "A bill of rights may be summed up in a few words. Why not write them down? Is it because it will consume too much paper?" Henry unabashedly attacked Madison's reticence to include a bill of rights by mocking the volumes of paper it would encompass. His friends were also critical. His political and personal mentor, Thomas Jefferson, strongly encouraged his protégé to introduce a bill of rights for the sake of the people and for the sake of the document. "A bill of rights is what the people are entitled to against every government on earth … and what no just government should refuse." The uproar among friend and foe was so boisterous, Madison understood he must listen to others if he wanted to accomplish his ultimate goal of ratifying the Constitution.

More often than not, leaders are met with multifaceted opposition to what they have personally laid out as the best-made plans. Yet, plans and ideas are only successful when the subjects of those plans are fully invested. To persuade others towards change and implementation, a leader must not only listen to friends, but they must also be *willing* to listen to critics and detractors to formulate the best story.

Salesforce Research recently surveyed over 1,500 business professionals on values-driven leadership and workplace equality. They reported that when an employee feels heard, that person is 4.6 times more likely to feel empowered to perform to the best of their abilities.[50] There is no more powerful way to "hear" an employee than to recount a story that directly illustrates their need for action.

In 1984, Steve Jobs introduced the first Macintosh computer at a shareholders meeting. Instead of a straightforward business pitch, he dramatically told a classic "good vs. evil" tale about the protagonist—Apple—and an antagonist—IBM. In the words of *Forbes* reporter Carmine Gallo:

> *Steve Jobs worked up the audience because he crafted the product in terms of good and evil, an irresistible combination. In the Steve Jobs narrative, the villain is a force that is aiming its guns at its last obstacle—the hero who is the last entity that can protect freedom. Is this a product launch or a script for a Star Wars-like movie? It's both, and that's why a Steve Jobs presentation was a mesmerizing experience. Jobs intuitively understood what great screenwriters know, what great works of literature are made of:*

heroes and villains are the fundamental building block of com-
pelling narrative.[51]

Steve Jobs' story not only invigorated the audience to embrace the
Macintosh computer, but also motivated a common investment in defend-
ing the story of the personal computer against competitors for generations.

If LBJ and James Madison failed to practice active listening towards the
anti-federalists in the 1700s and the burgeoning civil rights rhetoric of the
1950s, their ability to tell a compelling story about the need for civil rights
action and legislation would have been ineffective. Because they had honed
the skill of listening and storytelling, their power of persuasion moved
people to act and secured enduring changes to our federal government.

In the words of Bob Iger, "People still love a good story, and I don't
think that will change." People still love the personal computer—an
invention that was launched by a story. The experiences that shaped LBJ
and James Madison, retold and repackaged to address current need, illustrates the power of persuasion embedded in our own stories. Leaders
must include others in their story, in order to create a common narrative
that moves people to action and investment in a common purpose.

FROM TELEPHONE TO TWITTER—LEADERS UNDERSTAND THE MODERN TOOLS OF COMMUNICATION

One of the challenges of being a father has been learning to communicate with my three kids. I'm not talking about the normal par-
ent-to-angsty-teenager conversation. I'm talking about learning what
it means to interpret references like "ILYSM but I'm suffering FOMO
over Lizzo on Tik-Tok." I'm very interested in what they are saying but
often need an interpreter to find out if what they told me is really good,
really bad, or a new disease. And the main lesson I've learned is that
technology is moving so quickly, by the time I'm often on board, every-

one else has already jumped ship. (By the way, you can now search me on MySpace.)

Persuasion is impossible without effective communication.

Effective communication requires understanding and utilizing various communication tools—particularly the tools that are most common to the masses. And yes, that means using the words "tweet" and "Google" and "DM'd" as some of your favorite verbs. Persuasion through communication also involves body language, tone, and, according to Bridwell, "living our story every day in what we do, say, and repeat; personally and professionally."[52]

Lyndon Johnson was a master communicator. By far, one of his most effective tools of communication was his deliberate body language. There is an iconic photograph of LBJ towering over a much smaller Supreme Court Justice—Abe Fortas. This photograph has become the visual representation of what became known as the "Johnson Treatment." Utilizing his domineering physical stature, this tactic is described by newspaper columnist Mary McGrory as "an incredible, potent mixture of persuasion, badgering, flattery, threats, reminders of past favors and future advantages." LBJ was known to physically invade personal space. Combined with his mastery of detail and proficiency in the political process, he would then spare no time or tactic to persuade his subject to push through legislation or vote his way.

Lean In—Body Language Speaks Volumes

A poignant and seldom told example of the Johnson Treatment occurred after the passing of Medicare. Eighty-five percent of the public stood opposed to Medicare, bolstered by the vocal opposition of the American Medical Association. In response, Johnson invited the president of the AMA to the White House and asked if their organization would be willing to send doctors to serve the civilian population in Vietnam. When the AMA agreed, Johnson quickly arranged a press conference under the auspices of announcing publicly the incredible willingness of American doctors to travel to Vietnam to help those in need. When publicly asked during the press conference if the AMA would stand in the way of Medicare, Johnson responded, "These men are true patriots sending their doctors into Vietnam—of course they will uphold the law!" The AMA, under the pressure of the camera and their new commitment to sending doctors to Vietnam, were silenced. Johnson had successfully leveraged the moment to bully the AMA into his lane. A day later, 85 percent of the public adhered to Medicare, as opposed to the 85 percent dissention the day before. The AMA then vocalized support.

If body language were LBJ's primary tool, his secondary strategy was becoming a walking switchboard. LBJ was more connected than AT&T. He had mastered the telephone early on—installing phone lines throughout the White House and building an extensive phone network throughout his ranch to keep him accessible. He even figured out how to wire a phone to attach to an oak tree in his yard.[53] In the words of Mark Updegrove, "The best politicians of their time used the mediums of their times: Lincoln used the written word and early photography; FDR the radio; JFK the television; Obama harnessed social media; Trump with Twitter. During LBJ's presidency, people wrote and read. He used the power of personal interaction and a communication device—the telephone."

LBJ recorded approximately 9,000 phone calls during his presidency and was said to spend upwards of eighteen hours per day on the phone. He persuaded a lot of people via relentless phone conversations. Long before cellular phones that freed us to be reachable at any time and place, LBJ capitalized upon the latest ingenuity to construct a phone network that allowed him to remain more connected than any teenager in his day.

Leaders must become comfortable with the latest technology as a tool of effective communication and persuasion. During—and leading up to—his presidency, Madison was also on the cutting edge of communication technology, utilizing the power of the pen and the printing press. The printed newspaper was the equivalent of social media in the eighteenth century, and Madison became a top reporter. In the battle for ratification of the Constitution, those on both sides of the aisle were trying to make their messages go "viral." Yet it was Madison who set off a nineteenth century tweetstorm. Aside from Thomas Paine's writings— like *Common Sense*—no essays had a greater impact on persuading the public toward supporting the Constitution than *The Federalist Papers*. Called the "most important work of political philosophy in the history of our country," *The Federalist Papers* were written to convince a skeptical public of the value of this new Constitution using language and logic most people could understand. Madison leveraged a newspaper called *The Gazette of the United States* to continue seeking to sway the populace. Madison's use of his pen and these media outlets to persuade people, politicians, and governments rivals today's most ardent Twitter user. To paraphrase John Adams's comments about Thomas Paine—without the pen of Madison, the sword of George Washington might have been raised in vain.

Leaders who recognize the new, technological tools available to them—*and* overcome insecurity about learning a new medium—will find their power of persuasion exponentially enhanced.

Keep It Comin'—Leaders Communicate Consistently

In order for successful leaders to assure that their "swords are not raised in vain," they must adapt the flexibility and staffing to connect, communicate, and often manage from a distance via emerging media sources. And they must be consistent. I remember as a teenager going to hear my father speak to a large convention about "navigating the nineties." In an age when most presenters used overhead projectors, my dad was using computer presentations with software that would one day be transformed into PowerPoint. People were wowed at the amazing technology we all take for granted today. What is commonplace today was high tech back then and people still remind him of the impact that speech had on their lives. The content was great, but the technology used in the presentation made the message memorable.

Like LBJ and Madison, embracing the latest technology to its fullest potential increases the means of persuasion, and the opportunity to better connect with staff and management.

We live in the first digital generation in world history, and many people entering the workforce have never known an analog world. Communication changes have been fast, disruptive, and transformative. Leaders must be willing to engage social media to speak into the lives of upcoming generations. While much of social media is filled with cheap words and impulsive rhetoric, there is also unlimited space for communicating transformative, persuasive speech. Just as marketing departments are scrambling to create transformative social media campaigns, leaders also must adapt to the power of this medium for the purpose of shaping a new generation.

If you feel like the digital generation has passed you by and you are not adept at social media, let me encourage you to find someone to help you. You do not have to be the one "posting" every day, but make sure someone is representing you on the digital stage. Social media has become the pen, telephone, camera, and speech of today's generation, and leaders do not want to be absent from the conversation. Even as a pastor, I have found the importance of a variety of mediums to accomplish the vision and goals of an institution that is more than two millennia old. From face-to-face to Facebook, telephone calls to Instagram posts, our organization is always looking at new ways to communicate a timeless message.

LEADERS PURSUE A GREATER PURPOSE

As a college adjunct history professor, one of my favorite in-class discussions occurs when I give personal advice about the job interview process. As my students prepare to launch into the real world, their anxiety becomes less about their history grade and more about their job search. I always begin by offering advice on how to answer the first question—no matter what it is— in the interview. I suggest they respond, "That is a good question that I want to answer in a moment, but I would like to tell you about my vision for my life and how I think this job will help me accomplish that vision." This answer may not guarantee a job, but I do guarantee that the interviewer will remember how they answered the first question.

Foresight is 20/20—Leaders Have Clear Vision

Leaders must have vision and be driven by a greater purpose. Purpose is the engine that fuels the power of persuasion. The drive to accomplish a vision will empower others to find meaning and purpose in their work. When James Madison was elected the fourth President of the United States, his party was struggling, the nation was divided, and both France and Great Britain were threatening the newly formed republic. Yet, Madison took the oath of office, stating the purpose that brought him there and would sustain his presidency: "He would always prefer peaceful accommodations to war, he would support the Constitution, and he would be strengthened in these tasks by 'the well-tried intelligence and virtue of my fellow citizens.' In them he would place his confidence, 'next to that which we have all been encouraged to feel in the guardianship and guidance of that Almighty Being whose power regulates the destiny of nations.'"[54]

His unwavering dedication to the rights of individual liberties and freedoms was the driving purpose that had paved his road to the White

House. Earlier, motivated by the memories of the persecution of Baptists in Virginia, Madison was deeply committed to individual liberties—especially religious liberty. "Religious bondage shackles and debilitates the mind," he wrote to William Bradford, a college friend. This deep-seated belief in religious liberty for all (and particularly his passion about Virginia Baptists) would be a driving force in the first phrase of the First Amendment that the "Congress shall make no law respecting an establishment of religion, or prohibiting the free exercise thereof."

Almost two centuries later, LBJ stood in the shadow of the Bill of Rights and said, "We have talked long enough in this country about equal rights. We have talked for one hundred years or more. It is time now to write the next chapter, and to write it in the books of law." First Lady "Lady Bird" Johnson commented that her husband was born not seeing color. He determined early in his life to toe the line on segregation and Jim Crow ideology. But as with many people of that day, he began to see the error of his ways and the need to not only respect human dignity but advocate when he encountered oppression. His purpose, however, was shaped by these ideals, which in turn was the impetus for the "Great Society"—declaring a war on poverty, inequality, and bigotry. Not without flaws, LBJ was driven by a greater purpose. His decisions were guided by his favorite words from the Prophet Isaiah, "Come let us reason together." He had the ability to reason with the person on the other side, and to persuade them to embrace a higher purpose.

Leaders Distinguish Between Purpose and Goals

Purpose is much different than goal setting. Leaders must let their purpose drive their ongoing decisions, and that stated purpose becomes a shared vision that motivates teams to work towards common goals. Leaders must let others in on the overall purpose and culture of a company. The absence of purpose can lead to burnout and lack of vision for both the leader and those being led.

Many have neglected to contemplate a greater purpose—often buried under performance reviews, sales projections, budgetary pressures, or constant deadlines. Now is the time to reevaluate the reason that drives your work and the greater purpose for your actions. In the words of Mark Twain, "The two most important days in your life are the day you are born and the day you find out why." Through answering that "why," James Madison ultimately established the Bill of Rights and the provision for our individual liberties. It was the greater purpose of LBJ that seized this vision and gave it a strong voice through the Civil Rights Act of 1964. It is *your* vision that is necessary to continue the legacy of leadership that motivates and persuades others to action. We can all become the "good men (and women)" of whom Aristotle referred—individuals who are "absolutely true where exact certainty is impossible and opinions are divided."

Team Players

September 25, 1789, James Madison stood at center court while ten proposed amendments to the Constitution were adopted by the states. All of the listening, contemplating, theorizing, and writing culminated in a first-round victory called the Bill of Rights.

On July 2, 1964, President Johnson picked up the ball and, surrounded by a team of legislators, scribbled a sweeping championship of the pen to make the Civil Rights Act of 1964 a law. His action defeated discrimination in the workplace and provided for the integration of schools and public facilities. Like the first time Michael Jordan launched himself from the top of the key for a slam dunk, this was the loftiest civil rights legislation since the Reconstruction era.

James Madison and Lyndon Johnson differed in stature, temperament, erudition, and style. Their height differential was only eclipsed by the decibel level of their speech. Madison and Johnson were both able to reach new heights to push through transformational change. Their stories and styles have shaped generations, and we have all been equally drafted onto the same team.

Presidents traditionally leave a personal letter to their predecessor. One can say that #4 and #36 decided to share theirs with the entire country as they left office. Their power of persuasion, now realized in our Constitution and civil rights/health and welfare legislation is Madison and LBJ's last will and testament to all leaders: Tell compelling, personal stories. Use relevant communication. Pursue a greater life purpose. Eventually, you will convince those around you that life is full of great opportunities disguised as insoluble problems.

Chapter 9

Ronald Reagan & Woodrow Wilson

Leaders Unite

"America is not anything if it consists of each of us. It is something only if it consists of all of us."
–Woodrow Wilson

"Dr. Emmett Brown: Who's President of the United States in 1985?
Marty McFly: Ronald Reagan.
Dr. Emmett Brown: Ronald Reagan?! The actor?! Ha! Then who's vice president? Jerry Lewis?"
–Back to the Future

On June 12, 1987, President Ronald Reagan stood behind a podium at the base of the Brandenburg Gate in West Berlin poised to deliver one of his most memorable speeches. Directly challenging Mikhail Gorbachev, he dusted off his German and locked minds with the nemesis of the Cold War by peppering German phrases into his delivery. Behind him stretched eighty-seven miles of concrete and wire fence separating West Berlin from the eastern part of the city. German citizens stood in silent expectation as the president addressed the crowds, many of whom had been separated from their loved ones since the wall had been constructed in 1961.

> *There is one sign the Soviets can make that would be unmistakable, that would advance dramatically the cause of freedom and peace … Secretary General Gorbachev, if you seek peace—if you seek prosperity for the Soviet Union and Eastern Europe—if you seek liberalization: come here, to this gate.*
> *Mr. Gorbachev, open this gate!*
> *Mr. Gorbachev, tear down this wall!*[55]

That wall had been one of Germany's iconic symbols of oppression and, for Reagan, another barrier to eradicating communism. Forty years earlier, after the defeat of Germany in World War II, Berlin had been divided into four sections. The Americans, British, and French claimed control of the western region and the Soviets assumed communist power in the eastern region. These alliances ultimately shaped the borders of West and East Germany and, consequently, the Berlin Wall was built to prevent passage between the two sides and control the millions of East Germans attempting to flee the oppression.

The president, known for leading America through the Cold War, nostalgically recalled President Kennedy's speech two decades earlier. He then used his signature charm to draw the audience in further "Like so many presidents before me, I come here today because wherever I go, whatever I do: *Ich hab noch einen koffer in Berlin.*" Literally translated "I still have a suitcase in Berlin," the president made clear that his heart was with the city and his dedication to follow up on his challenge to Gorbachev and uniting Berlin was unquestioned. To seal his call to unity, his voice rang passionately over the 20,000 in attendance: *"Es gibt nur ein Berlin!"*—There is only one Berlin!

BACK TO THE FUTURE—LEADERS UNITE

Had President Ronald Reagan hopped in Marty McFly's space-traveling DeLorean and arrived at the White House in 1921, he would have had a lot to say to President Woodrow Wilson. He would have definitely discussed his Berlin speech and agreed to disagree with Wilson's hope for fair treatment of Russia as the "acid test" of his post-World War I global peace initiative. President Reagan then may have challenged Wilson's treatment of socialists after the war and how that may have ultimately contributed to the Cold War he was confronting sixty years in the future. Reagan would have given Wilson a nod for the passage of the Federal Reserve Act and described how his own Federal Reserve Chairman used that post to tighten interest rates to reign in the rampant inflation and recession that had crippled the country. On a personal note, Wilson—who often made self-deprecating jokes about his looks—may have noted that presidents in the future were as stunningly good looking as actors. And both would acknowledge that nothing had really changed in the Office of the First Lady where both of their second wives had no problem bending their ear and influencing decisions. Wilson would smile that he commissioned the first film ever screened in the White House. Reagan would laugh that he was the first actor they let in the West Wing. Finally, before climbing back in the DeLorean to return to his wrangling with the Soviet Union, President Reagan would have clapped Wilson on the shoulder and assured him that his efforts to form a League of Nations and usher in worldwide peace were not in vain. He would encourage him to stay the course, and to assure him that the United Nations had been ultimately established to unite countries thanks to his groundwork. Wilson, feeling some relief from the acrimony surrounding his ideas for peace, would have shaken Reagan's hand and asked him to carry on the work he could not accomplish in his lifetime. Reagan—with his iconic wit—would have nodded and said he'd "win one for the Gipper!"

While presidents #28 and #40 didn't meet in history, they definitely were comrades in uniting others—past, present, and future.

We Are the World

In January of 1985, some of America's top recording artists slipped quietly into A&M Recording Studios in Hollywood directly following the American Music Awards. They were greeted by the sign PLEASE CHECK YOUR EGOS AT THE DOOR[56] as they embarked upon an all-night recording session led by Stevie Wonder, Michael Jackson, and Quincy Jones. The vocalists and choir united a diverse group of forty-six solo artists ranging from pop sensation Cyndi Lauper to country's Willie Nelson. When the session wrapped, the team had successfully recorded the song "We Are the World" that topped music charts and became the first single to be certified multiplatinum. The purpose of the single, and the album by that name, was not the notoriety of the performers. They gathered in an effort to raise money and awareness for the benefit of humanitarian aid—particularly in Ethiopia following the recent famine that had claimed over one million lives. Had word gotten out, or one of the many personalities in the room sought a different outcome, the project could have been a disaster. Instead, it was an international success thanks to a clearly stated objective and the common commitment to that goal.

This high-profile, worthy effort is a reflection of the unity brought about by the leadership of both President Wilson and President Reagan. They had no problem drawing together some of the world's most contentious leaders to usher in democracy and relief from war and nuclear threat. Their efforts to unite big personalities and demand they "leave their egos at the door" set the stage for the creation of the United Nations and the end of the Cold War.

Star Wars

When Ronald Reagan became president in 1981, the country was weighed down by inflation, high unemployment, and a general low-grade fever of despair. The president immediately began to speak with exuberance about a vision for a restored America that would rise as a shining city on a hill. He was able to unite the public around its desire to believe that there were better days ahead. He kept his vision simple, focusing on two primary objectives: reinvigorate the economy and bring communism and the nuclear threat to an end. In his words,

> *"Our country is a special place, because we Americans have always been sustained, through good times and bad, by a noble vision—a vision not only of what the world around us is today but what we as a free people can make it be tomorrow."*

Along with revitalizing the economy, President Reagan spent most of his presidency redefining the United States' relationship with the Soviet Union. Once calling the USSR the "evil empire" and the "focus of evil in the modern world," Reagan was concerned that the amassing of nuclear weapons by the Soviets, and the inadequate SALT II Treaty crafted under Carter, left the United States exposed. Reagan cast a vision for a world free of the threat of nuclear weapons and continually went after the Soviet Union in order to forge a peace agreement.

He unveiled a plan to build a missile defense system that included a space shield to shelter the United States from incoming missiles. The system was nicknamed "Star Wars" after the George Lucas film popular during that era. He also set out to combat the Soviet-supported Marxist regimes globally. This included Afghanistan after the Soviet invasion, El

Salvador, Cuba, and Nicaragua. According to the Miller Center at the University of Virginia:

> *To Reagan, the soldiers and insurgents struggling against Communism on battlefields throughout the world were "freedom fighters," a description he particularly applied to the Contras opposing the Sandinista government in Nicaragua. In his February 6, 1985, State of the Union message, Reagan called for support of anti-Communist forces "from Afghanistan to Nicaragua" and proclaimed that "support for freedom fighters is self-defense."*[57]

Reagan used any means and reached past geographical boundaries to fight communism and forge a new relationship with the Soviet Union. Using his rhetoric skills and his innate ability to feed off the temperature of the pubic regarding the threat the Soviet Union posed, Reagan united the country in a common belief that the breakdown of communism and the shake-up of the Soviet Union was necessary for a peaceful, nuclear-free world. In 1983, *Time* magazine featured President Reagan and Soviet leader Yuri Andropov on its year-end cover, naming them both "Men of the Year." National news had formally concurred that President Reagan had made his intentions to combat communism and defeat the nuclear threat very clear. British Prime Minister Margaret Thatcher commented: "Let us above all thank President Reagan for ending the West's retreat from world responsibility, for restoring the pride and leadership of the United States, and for giving the West back its confidence. He has left America stronger, prouder, greater than ever before."[58]

In December 2013, General Motors announced its first female CEO—Mary Barra. Barra had worked at GM for thirty-three years in engineering, product manufacturing, and management. As she assumed her role and rolled out her plan as head of the company, Barra set clear objectives by casting a vision to compete with cars like Tesla. "The good news is that our generation has the ambition, the talent, and the technology to realize the safer, better, and more sustainable world we want. General Motors has committed itself to leading the way toward this future, guided by our vision of zero crashes, zero emissions, and zero congestion."[59]

Like Reagan, Barra had cast a sweeping vision with very clear, simple, well-stated objectives: zero crashes, zero emissions, and zero congestion. While critics have weighed in, highlighting her shortcomings with this plan, it is a vision she is passionate about achieving. She continues to propel GM into the electric car space and fight for these initiatives.[60]

In the same way, leaders must cast a clear vision to motivate unity. There may be multiple challenges in the organization, but, like Reagan, set your focus on the ones that can unite your team, and narrow your goals. For President Reagan, his vision was to restore the economy and end communism. For Barra, it is the production of electric vehicles over internal combustion cars. Both leaders have made the vision simple to understand, and then worked to develop loyalty and commitment to that shared vision.

For your organization, you must decide what that clear vision is that will unify your team.

And on a personal note, the same is true for how you lead within your family. Teams, and families for that matter, do not unify around three-ring binders of long-term, strategic plans. Rather, it is the bold, simple vision that unites people together.

A Common Objective

At the end of World War I, the nation—and those abroad—viewed President Wilson as a world hero. The president, who had earlier resisted bringing the United States into a conflict that had already cost fourteen million European lives, ultimately led the nation into World War I and then to victory. Like Reagan, Wilson had a vision for a world at peace and the global end of totalitarianism. He viewed the postwar period as his perfect opportunity to realize his idealism. Earlier in the war, he had laid the foundation of this vision to make the world safe for democracy:

> *The world must be made safe for democracy. Its peace must be planted upon the tested foundations of political liberty. We have no selfish ends to serve. We desire no conquest, no dominion. We seek no indemnities for ourselves, no material compensation for the sacrifices we shall freely make.*

> –On the state of war with Germany during
> an address to Congress. April 2, 1917.

Wilson then outlined his "Fourteen Points" upon which lasting peace could be accomplished through eradication of secret treaties and a "new diplomacy." One of his fourteen points was the creation of a League of Nations formed under specific covenants for the purpose of affording mutual guarantees of political independence and territorial integrity. He travelled with a delegation to the Paris Peace Conference in order to solidify this treaty—which represents the first time a president had traveled to Europe. He was greeted as a hero and credited for ending the bloody war that had cost so many lives. Ultimately, by the end of the trip, the resulting Treaty of Versailles looked very little like Wilson's ideals and objectives. However, Wilson stayed the course, embarking on a twenty-nine-city speaking tour in an attempt to unite the country around his ideals by igniting the fight against the common enemy of war and authoritarian regimes. While Wilson was ultimately unsuccessful in convincing America to join the League of Nations, he did set a tone for the pursuit of world peace and the fight against the common enemy of despotism and war.

Not long ago, our office had a contest we named after the television show *The Biggest Loser*. Similar to the show, several staff members volunteered for this friendly competition to see who could lose the most weight by percentage. The contest was designed to improve the overall health of our employees and included a financial incentive and an extra week of vacation for the winners. What was interesting was how the competition was never one employee versus another—it was all of our employees versus foods that pack on the pounds. Everyone cheered each other on throughout those weeks and there was a definite feeling that if you were going to eat something that wasn't good for you, you probably needed to keep it a secret. Our team joined together in a fierce competition—not with each other, but with our common enemy: the calorie.

According to the Air Force doctrine, "Unity of command is one of the principles of war … This principle emphasizes that all efforts should be directed and coordinated toward a common objective." [61] For Wilson, the common enemy was totalitarianism and threat of war. Thus the enemies of his enemy became friends.

LEADERS STRATEGICALLY COMMUNICATE TO UNITE PEOPLE

In 2014 and 2015, Elizabeth Holmes—the youngest female self-styled billionaire—was on top of the world. Appearing on the cover of *Forbes, Time, Inc., Fortune* and *Glamour* magazines, this female phenom was poised to revolutionize the health care world. Dropping out of Stanford at age nineteen, she started the company Theranos, which claimed it could replace traditional viniculture by performing blood tests utilizing only one drop of blood collected by a pinprick of the finger. No more needles and painful blood draws, she claimed. Courting investors such as Warren Buffet, former Secretary of State George Schulz, Betsy DeVoss, and former Defense Secretary Jim Mattis, Holmes spoke in her signature baritone voice and mesmerized her audience with her uncharacteristically low voice and her unblinking eyes. Transfixed by her bold communication style, the country was poised to welcome the next revolutionary IPO to the market. Elizabeth Holmes had successfully united people from all walks of life with her story about revolutionizing common blood draws—a procedure familiar to all, and disdained by most.

Until it all came crashing down, that is. Thanks to the bravery of a few whistleblowers within the company, Elizabeth Holmes was exposed as this generation's biggest fraud, bilking investors out of millions of dollars. The technology didn't work, the results of the blood test had been doctored, and Elizabeth Holmes had even doctored her voice to appear more masculine than it really was. The master communicator, whose story was sold to the nation's most wealthy investors, had powerfully united people hopeful for a better way. Ultimately, both her voice and her platform were inauthentic and the truth came to light. For leaders, good communication *must* be partnered with the truth.

The Voice

All charismatic leaders find their "voice" and become known for their distinct style of communicating. Reagan, known as the "Great Communicator" was great, and not just because of his unique voice. He was great because he was able to effectively communicate what he really believed to be true and what he ultimately planned to deliver. Unlike Elizabeth Holmes, Reagan harnessed the power of communication as an outgrowth of his firm convictions and his vision for America. His transparency and ability to draw in his audience with his signature warmth and humor broke down more walls than just the one in Berlin. Reagan once said, "Most often it's not how handsomely or eloquently you say something, but the fact that your words mean something." His words were meaningful, his delivery was masterful, and his vision was magnetic. According to David Hancock, author of *State of the Union: A Tribute to Ronald Reagan:*

> Ronald Reagan believed that everything happened for a reason, and that we can trust in God's purposes. He believed that people are basically good. He had no tolerance for bigotry or injustice. Above all, he believed in the courage and triumph of free men and in the capacity of the American people to overcome any obstacle. With bold, persistent action, he restored the confidence of our nation, strengthened the spirit of free enterprise, challenged and shamed an oppressive empire, and inspired millions with his conviction and moral courage. As he showed what a president should be, he also showed us what a man should be. Ronald Reagan carried himself with a decency and attention to the small kindnesses that also define a good life. He was a courtly, gentle, and considerate man, never known to slight or embarrass others. Ronald Reagan deeply loved the United States of America. And that love was returned.

Best-selling author, coach, and speaker John Maxwell has a lot to say about authenticity of voice and conviction in leadership. In his blog, he outlines how to unite others under authenticity. In his view, leaders must: define authenticity, channel their own self-awareness, and find common ground. He writes, "More than a strategic keyword that you weave into your resume, 'authenticity' should live at the intersection of corporate leadership development and business outcomes."[62]

Over the years of my life, I have discovered that every age group values authenticity, but I have also learned the upcoming generation of leaders seems to value it more. It is ironic that the generation that has been raised on a steady diet of perfect social media posts is the one that craves authenticity the most. Perhaps the deluge of phoniness they see on social media makes them long for something real, true, and authentic. What a great opportunity for the older generation to connect with the young leaders by encouraging authenticity in their leadership style and mentoring them to that end.

Developing and honing an authentic "voice" is essential in uniting others around a common vision and ensuring that vision speaks even after your tenure is over.

The Last Laugh

It is no secret that President Reagan was a master at comic delivery. On March 31, 1981, Reagan was shot in the chest outside a Washington D.C. hotel. The bullet had come within an inch of his heart. While on the operating table, he famously quipped, "I just hope you are all Republicans." And to his wife, "I forgot to duck." First appearing to Congress after his recovery, he quoted a letter he received from a child in the second grade, "I hope you get well quick, or you might have to make a speech in your pajamas." This line brought the house down and softened the fear of another assassination attempt. His signature humor deflected many tense and contentious moments over the years.

During his 1984 Presidential debate with Walter Mondale, Reagan addressed the issue of his age—as he was the oldest United States President to date. He said, "I will not make age an issue of this campaign. I am not going to exploit, for political purposes, my opponent's youth and inexperience." Even his opponent, Walter Mondale, erupted with laughter. Reagan was able to then move forward with his unifying message "It's Morning in America Again" and continue leading his campaign to victory.

Laughter is a great tool in the arsenal of any leader. When well-timed, it diffuses tense situations, puts the audience at ease, and opens minds to new possibilities that may have been closed by prejudice and tradition. Mark Twain once wrote, "Against the assault of laughter, nothing can stand." Walter Mondale understood that. Reagan won the election by a landslide.

As leaders, if laughter is in your arsenal, use it sparingly but use it well.

Just as important as humor are well-placed illustrations—particularly spoken during times of solemn attention—to unite those you lead. While speaking at Normandy to commemorate the fortieth anniversary of D-Day, President Reagan emotionally used the occasion not only to honor the "boys of Point-du-hoc," but also illustrate that the fight against totalitarianism during World War II is the same Cold War struggle against totalitarianism in the present day.

> *The men of Normandy had faith that what they were doing was right, faith that they fought for all humanity, faith that a just God would grant them mercy on this beachhead or on the next. It was the deep knowledge—and pray God we have not lost it—that there is a profound, moral difference between the use of force for liberation and the use of force for conquest.*

Called one of his more masterful speeches, President Reagan used the moment to rally all Americans to recommit to fighting for democracy and opposing communism and weapons of mass destruction. Reagan consistently harnessed these moments to advance his vision while maintaining the authenticity of his compassion for the present circumstance.

There are many opportunities in any organization to read the situation and the crowd, and utilize the tools of humor or illustration to address the need at hand, while still building the bonds of united effort. Do not let these opportunities pass you by, but embrace the moments to unite one another under a common cause. And whatever you do, mean what you say.

LEADERS UNITE THROUGH THE MOST COMMON DENOMINATOR

It is my great privilege every week to stand before a wide range of people to share a message of hope from the Bible. If you know much about churches, you know they are often more diverse than people realize. I speak to people literally from ages nine to ninety-nine who not only come from different backgrounds and experiences, but also dramatically different ways of viewing the world. A child of the Great Depression views the world differently than someone from the "Me Generation" of the 1980s or the evolving digital generation. In order to effectively "shepherd a flock," you have to speak to the common denominator. Thankfully, I have the best subject each week and I'm not out there on my own. But I must always be sensitive to my audience and make sure I'm speaking in a way that connects with all generations, whether they grew up on Andy Griffith, Andy Gibb, or Andy Grammer.

Tragedy and Triumph—When Everyone is Listening

I remember sitting in my high school history class as an announcement came over the intercom. The principal informed our school about the tragic explosion of the Space Shuttle Challenger. I happened to be in one of the few classes with a television and my teacher turned it on. To this day, I can clearly "hear" the silence in that room. Some of you may have a similar recollection.

Following the Challenger explosion on January 28, 1986, President Reagan became one of our first "pastors in chief" by scrapping his State of the Union speech and addressing a nation in shock and mourning. In his televised address delivered from his desk, he solemnly acknowledged the tragedy while still upholding the importance of the space program and those dedicated to space exploration. He illustrated how those seven who perished had been endowed with "special grace, a hunger to explore, and a desire to serve," honoring their families and loved ones. He then turned and looked straight at the camera to address the schoolchildren who had been watching the launch and spoke into their grief and confusion. Knowing that his words would cut to the heart of the adults listening too, he spoke through childlike eyes about the pain and confusion of tragedy, and offered hope for tomorrow. By speaking to the youngest—as everyone has a common understanding of youth—the president was able to comfort the entire nation while still confirming that space exploration was important and must continue—even that more teachers would eventually go into space.

There is nothing more powerful than addressing the "*most* common denominator" in the room, in order to simplify and verify what everyone else needs to hear. It is the most humble approach, and the most powerful position. For leaders, it demonstrates an ability to relate, and to care about the participation of everyone involved, not just the most evolved. Scan the audience, find the commonality, and unite others around what is shared.

Unity is Not Uniformity

When Richard Nixon took office, he returned President Woodrow Wilson's desk to the Oval Office as a statement of unity. He saw himself as an extension of Wilson's legacy, endeavoring to bring about a new world order during the rise of the Cold War. President Wilson's legacy in envisioning the League of Nations and a world that could work together in its diversity to usher in peace and democracy has had a lasting impact worldwide.

> Wilson's most important proposal was the prevention of future wars by means of a new international organization, a League of Nations, open to membership by all democratic states. This new world body would be in charge of disarmament and the dismantling of colonial possessions. Most importantly, the League would hold power over all disputes among its members. Wilson believed that this League would transform international relations and usher in a new era of world peace.[63]

President Wilson's firm belief that unity did not require uniformity, but rather, that differences could unite and complement a common vision, transformed world relations. Although he was unsuccessful in his presidency—and lifetime—to implement this vision, it did come to fruition on October 24, 1945, when the United Nations Charter was ratified by the United States of America, China, France, the Soviet Union, the United Kingdom, and the other member states. Wilson understood that peace would be the uniting factor for a diversity of governments and personalities—and that it would possibly become a future reality.

As a history teacher, every semester is a multicultural experience. The university where I teach has many international students and they are always a delight to get to know. Recently at a faculty training, I attended a panel discussion of three international students who offered their advice for professors teaching students from other countries. I was reminded as I listened to them of the strength that comes as cultures cross paths. I am a better instructor because I teach students from other cultures, and hopefully they are better students through their encounters with me. Those students bring insight and perspective I would otherwise miss. Although we come from different places around the globe, the common bond of humanity makes us all better people.

Leaders who learn to embrace diversity while uniting under a common vision have the opportunity for sweeping, robust cooperation and the benefit of alternative viewpoints and styles. In the words of Harry Potter, "We are only as strong as we are united, as weak as we are divided."

Back from the Future—Unity Endures

President Woodrow Wilson left the White House physically ill, discouraged, and defeated. His great League of Nations vision for which he had traveled to twenty-nine cities in three weeks, left him exhausted and bedridden for the rest of his tenure. He died without realizing the outcome of his efforts to unite the world under a flag of freedom and democracy.

Had he been able to step into that time-traveling DeLorean with President Reagan, he would have been revitalized traveling through the forties to observe how President Roosevelt took up the torch and spearheaded the creation of the United Nations after World War II. Traveling on, he would have enjoyed spirited discussions with Reagan about the rise of the Cold War and whether his treatment of socialists in 1920s America may have contributed to the problem. Stepping out into the Oval Office, he would have requested he sit at his old desk and share their common vision about how to contain oppressive ideologies and ultimately eradicate communism from the face of the earth. Then Reagan, with his signature wit, would have lightened the mood with one of his self-deprecating, Soviet Union jokes—probably the one he told to Gorbachev himself:

> *An American and Russian were arguing about their two countries.*
> *The American said: "Look, in my country, I can walk right into the Oval Office, pound the president's desk, and say, 'Mr. President, I don't like the way you are running this country!'"*
> *The Russian said: "I can do that!"*
> *The American answered: "You can?"*
> *The Russian said: "Yes. I can go into the Kremlin, to the general secretary's office, pound his desk and say, 'Mr. Secretary, I don't like the way President Reagan is running his country!'"*

After a hearty laugh, they would both hop into the DeLorean, step out at the crumbling Berlin Wall on November 9, 1989, and applaud President George H. W. Bush who ultimately was the one who solidified their vision in history. Their united vision, built on their convictions, communicated with precision and clarity, survived generations and ultimately became a reality under someone else's watch. Because they left their ego at the door, their vision endured and united future generations.

Be a leader who unites. Embrace diversity. Communicate with clarity, humor, and passion. Leave your ego at the door and your vision will endure. And if that united vision does not become a reality during your tenure, just remember the words of Marty McFly: "I guess you guys aren't ready for that yet. But your kids are gonna love it!"

Chapter 10

John F. Kennedy & Barack Obama

Leaders Inspire

"If you build it, he will come."
–Field of Dreams

"After all, a lot of people are going to think we are a shocking pair."
–Sidney Poitier in *Guess Who's Coming to Dinner*

On October 16, 1901, educator and former slave, Booker T. Washington was invited by President Theodore Roosevelt to join him for dinner at the White House. This dinner invitation was a dilemma for Washington as it marked the first time an African American man had been invited to share a meal at the table of the President of the United States. Both Roosevelt and Washington confronted

151

the hesitation they felt, and both men boldly stepped up to the dinner plate. While not a complete home run, the event took a swing at a moral, legal, and political dilemma that was continuing to plague the country—segregation and racial inequality. The South was outraged by the guest list. The bold implication of social equality suggested by that 1901 dinner party left the nation divided and in shock. Many vowed to never vote for Teddy Roosevelt again and the Southern press relentlessly criticized the president and his wife. As for President Roosevelt, he decided to make a bold public statement: "I shall have him dine as often as I please." However, the backlash had set a precedent and his words ultimately rang hollow. It was three decades before another person of color dined at a president's table.

Sixty years later, segregation was still plaguing the South with little movement from the White House. Just a few weeks before the 1960 presidential election, Dr. Martin Luther King was arrested while staging protests in Atlanta. It was the intervention of presidential candidate John F. Kennedy and his brother Robert Kennedy that established King's release—and put race and civil rights on the front burner of the president-elect's desk. Newly elected President Kennedy began setting his dinner table with a new era of Civil Rights initiatives. Three years into his presidency, during the controversial admission of two black students at the University of Alabama, President John F. Kennedy decided to make a bold public statement and addressed the nation:

> *The rights of every man are diminished when the rights of one man are threatened. Today we are committed to a worldwide struggle to promote and protect the rights of all who wish to be free ... We are confronted with a moral issue ... next week I shall ask the Congress of the United States to act to make a commitment it has not fully made in this century to the proposition that race has no place in American life or law.*[64]

Later in that year, the Civil Rights Bill garnered support of House and Senate Republicans, but it was not passed before the shocking assassination of President Kennedy on November 22, 1963. The fate of the African American man hung in the balance as the inspiring young president who had stepped up to the plate, had taken his last swing at the problem.

Another four decades passed. Then, seemingly out of nowhere, a young, charismatic black man emerged on the roster of presidential candidates. His words sparked a fire, his vision provided clarity, and his courage inspired voters like never before. On November 4, 2008, the Barack Obama family took the stage in Grant Park, Chicago, to the deafening cheers of a quarter million people. The president-elect stepped up to the podium, confidently making a bold public statement as the camera panned a very emotional, multicultural audience. His presence, rising behind the microphone, left little doubt that Roosevelt's dinner, and the assassinations of Kennedy and King did not succeed in silencing their voices.

If there is anyone out there who still doubts that America is a place where anything is possible, who still wonders if the dream of our founders is alive in our time, who still questions the power of our democracy, tonight is your answer.
–Barack Obama, Election Night 2008

Families clasped each other and stared at the young African American family standing before them. All eyes were drawn to the Obama daughters and the strong wife and mother who stood confidently by their side. Both young and older Americans pushed towards the stage, understanding that the days of sitting in the back of the bus were over. In the words of CBS News anchor Katie Couric, "No matter who you voted for, you'd have to agree—this is an incredible milestone in the history of this country." And Tom Brokaw weighed in from his news desk, capturing the moment for the American people. "This is a very emotional moment for everyone in this country, and for the world for that matter. This is not just a moment in American history, this is a profoundly important passage out of our deep shadows of our racist past that began with that first slave loaded on a ship. Race has been a curse for America for a long time. We are working our way through it."[65]

For the next eight years, there would be an African American man dining nightly at the White House, not as a guest, but as the *host* of the presidential meals. The dinner tables had turned, and those who used to play host and hostess, were the ones who now had to check the guest list. America had invited its first black president to preside over the table set by John F. Kennedy and so many who came before him.

The inspirational efforts of #35 and #44 is like pairing a tart dessert with a satisfying meal. While some might find them a shocking pair, their presidencies complement and amplify the accomplishments of each other.

LEADERS INSPIRE OTHERS TO DREAM

In 1989, the fantasy sports film *Field of Dreams* arrived in America's theaters to great critical acclaim. This story is about an Iowa farmer, Ray Kinsella, who hears a voice saying "If you build it, he will come." Ray obediently cuts down his cornfield, and in spite of the taunts of skeptics, builds a baseball field. Along the way, he hears other messages to "go the distance" and "ease your pain." Suddenly, the ghosts of great players show up at his newly constructed diamond to play ball, celebrating the game of baseball. It eventually becomes clear, however, that the message of the movie is also meant for Ray—for him to "go the distance" and to "ease his pain" as he ends up playing catch with his own father. The message of the film is for everyone, and it is also for him. When Ray seeks advice from writer Terrance Mann, this is how Mann responds:

People will come, Ray ... And they'll walk out to the bleach-
ers, sit in shirtsleeves on a perfect afternoon. They'll find they
have reserved seats somewhere along one of the baselines, where
they sat when they were children and cheered their heroes. And
they'll watch the game and it'll be as if they dipped themselves
in magic waters. The memories will be so thick they'll have
to brush them away from their faces. People will come, Ray.
The one constant through all the years, Ray, has been baseball.
America has rolled by like an army of steamrollers. It has been
erased like a blackboard, rebuilt and erased again. But baseball
has marked the time. This field, this game: it's a part of our
past, Ray. It reminds us of all that once was good and it could
be again. Oh ... people will come, Ray. People will most defi-
nitely come.[66]

Ray Kinsella was inspired to dream, and when he acted upon it, its impact did not just heal him, it healed the masses that were drawn to his dream. People will most definitely come to leaders who dream.

Risky Business

In his book *Dreams of My Father: A Story of Race and Inheritance*, President Obama writes about the leaders that shaped him and freed him to tell his story. These early influences essentially opened the door to dreaming bigger dreams and connecting him to others in a more meaningful way: "That's what the leadership was teaching me, day by day: that the self-interest I was supposed to be looking for extended well beyond the immediacy of issues, that beneath the small talk and sketchy biographies and received opinions, people carried with them some central explanation of themselves. Stories full of terror and wonder, studded with events that still haunted or inspired them. Sacred stories."[67]

Like Ray Kinsella, President Obama first opened his life to other stories, and then was masterful at fusing his dreams with the hopes of others. He overcame his reticence to share his background and the unusual journey that had brought him to Chicago. He risked his reputation, and in the process, opened the playing field to others who felt the same way. His rise to the presidency didn't just heal the racial and identity issues he had faced his whole life, it brought millions along with him, inspiring their dreams too. He learned to listen to stories about health care and incarceration, about economic and racial strife. Those stories caused him to dream big dreams about change. To dream is to risk—it's the risk that if you build it, they will not come. But risk-takers find that more often, they do.

Few leaders have taken more personal risks and instilled more people with clear vision than Dr. Martin Luther King. From his "I Have a Dream" speech, to his Montgomery bus boycott, to his March on Washington, King was a master at communicating his vision, stepping out in personal vulnerability and following up with concrete action. He consistently shared his vision and gave the masses new dreams and new vision themselves.

Leaders must take personal risk—which often includes the risk of being labeled as "crazy" or making some people uncomfortable—in order to inspire the dreams of others. For president-elect John F. Kennedy, it was a phone call to Dr. King's wife, and subsequently the governor of Alabama, that put him in personal peril of losing the presidential election as he took a stand for Martin Luther King. In the words of his brother, Bobby Kennedy, "Do you know," he [Bobby Kennedy] fumed, "that three Southern governors told us that if Jack supported Jimmy Hoffa, Nikita Khrushchev, or Martin Luther King, they would throw their states to Nixon? Do you know that this election may be razor close and you have probably lost it for us?"[68]

This enormous risk did not, in fact, nullify his chances for president.

At the final count, his risk ended up bringing a whole new electorate to his side to dream new dreams and solidify his victory. Kennedy took the risk, and the people did come.

Shoe Dog

The autobiography *Shoe Dog* is the long-awaited memoir of the founder and shoe titan of Nike, Phil Knight. A college student who always loved sports, Knight recognized himself as an entrepreneur while in a business class at Stanford. Marrying his love of sports, his interest in better, foreign shoes, and his business mind, he set out to change the running world by offering new footwear. Partnering with his old running coach at the University of Oregon, Bill Bowerman, Knight sparked a growing dream of the impossible—dominate the sports footwear world one shoe at a time. There were many critics who told Knight a guy like him could never build a shoe empire. But Knight believed the impossible. One of the great keys to his success was a lesson he learned from General Patton:

"Don't tell people how to do things. Tell them what to do and let them surprise you with their results."

And he would tell the youth who aspired to dream the impossible, to first seek a calling. Only then, the energy and faith required to dream impossible dreams would come:

"I'd tell men and women in their mid-twenties not to settle for a job or a profession or even a career. Seek a calling. Even if you don't know what that means, seek it. If you're following your calling, the fatigue will be easier to bear, the disappointments will be fuel, the highs will be like nothing you've ever felt." [69]

Leaders who want to inspire others to dream of the impossible and act upon those dreams must first give them the freedom to seek a calling, and then the encouragement to do their job with personal creativity and ownership. Impossible dreams come to fruition with motivated, inspired teams who make the impossible their calling.

One Giant Leap for Mankind

As JFK assumed the presidency, it was widely believed that the Russians were beating the United States in the race to be the first to dominate space programs. Kennedy set out to achieve what most thought was impossible—land a man on the moon. The president seized the opportunity to speak to a crowd at Rice University while on a visit to view the site that would house the new manned spacecraft center. Known as his "We Choose to Go to the Moon" speech, Kennedy inspired over 40,000 listeners to choose to lift their minds to what is possible:

> *"We choose to go to the moon. We choose to go to the moon in this decade and do the other things, not because they are easy, but because they are hard, because that goal will serve to organize and measure the best of our energies and skills, because that challenge is one that we are willing to accept, one we are unwilling to postpone, and one which we intend to win, and the others, too."*[70]

Inspiring others to embrace impossible dreams means coming clean on what it takes to achieve them: hard work, goals, energy and skill, and a willingness to accept a challenge. JFK set the tone of inspiration. The groundwork was laid at the new manned space facility in Houston and the work was carried out long after he was assassinated. Kennedy launched the nation into a giant leap forward—and by doing so, passed the baton to 40,000 others. On July 16, 1968, five years after Kennedy's death, Apollo 11 left the Kennedy Space Center. By the evening of July

20, Neil Armstrong stepped out onto the moon. The impossible became possible, because the president had the courage to dream and the ability to inspire.

It has been said that we all have the power to inspire others, or conversely, make them only perspire. When you transform impossible dreams into action, you will "serve to organize and measure the best of your team's energy and skills," and turn their perspiration into inspiration.

LEADERS INSPIRE WITH BOTH POSITIVITY AND REALISM

During President Obama's first term in office, the rate of Americans living without health insurance hit an all-time high at 18.2 percent. In addition, rising health care costs were straining businesses and employees, causing many to choose to be uninsured in order to feed their families. The insurance companies had the right to cancel health insurance for any reason, even in the midst of a sickness, and many were filing for bankruptcy protection due to the out-of-pocket costs of long-term care needs. Very few Americans were immune to the reality of a health care crisis. Many attempts had been made to revamp the health care system in America over the years, but few had even come close to addressing the problems. Financially, this was the single most devastating crisis for many families. President Obama listened to the stories from young and old, and responded to the nation with a plan.

Do Something—Leaders Act Within Their Reality

Citing many personal stories of citizens who had suffered with health insurance issues, President Obama boldly announced new legislation called the Affordable Care Act—commonly known as *Obamacare*—to address this problem and offer a sweeping solution. However, he did not present this to the country as an initiative that would expect a quick win or nod of popularity. He interjected his description of the solution, with the realistic warning that sweeping change of this magnitude would not come easily, nor avoid opposition, challenges, and setbacks.

> *Now, that doesn't mean that it's [Affordable Care Act] perfect. No law is. And it's true that a lot of the noise around the health care debate, ever since we tried to pass this law, has been nothing more than politics. But we've also always known—and I have always said—that for all the good that the Affordable Care Act is doing right now—for as big a step forward as it was—it's still just a first step. It's like building a starter home—or buying a starter home. It's a lot better than not having a home, but you hope that over time you make some improvements. And in fact, since we first signed the law, we've already taken a number of steps to improve it. And we can do even more—but only if we put aside all the politics, rhetoric, all the partisanship, and just be honest about what's working, what needs fixing and how we fix it. So that's what I want to do today. This isn't kind of a rah-rah speech.*[71]

To this day, I am certain that the mention of the word "Obamacare" is not being met with indifference or any sort of "rah-rah speech." But President Obama did demonstrate that inspiration to change a flawed system must be met with realism and the attitude that we must do something about it. In the words of the president, "What matters isn't the size of the step you take. What matters is that you take it."

As a leader, it is not enough to point out the problem. The only way to inspire others towards a solution is to act, or provide the platform for others to act within appropriate parameters. To be honest about the reality of a situation often gives more clarity on what challenges lie ahead and the perseverance required once action has been taken.

When my daughter was in fifth grade, we walked through some very difficult days. For a number of months, she had sharp pains in her back that felt as if she were being stabbed by an ice pick. At times, she could hardly walk and her fear of the stabbing pain at any moment was paralyzing. Doctors were unable to diagnose the cause of this terrible, crippling pain.

Finally, after four months of frustration, testing, and countless tears, the doctors decided to do exploratory surgery on her spinal cord. While we trusted the skilled doctors, our daughter looked to us as parents to help her navigate what she was facing. The fact she was an intelligent young lady both helped us and hurt us. I found myself trying to balance the reality of what the doctors were telling us as parents and the risks she really needed to know. As you probably are aware, being mentally strong is a vital ingredient to dealing with chronic pain, and I wanted to make sure I was giving her the facts, but not so many details as to break her spirit. In the same way, leaders have to constantly walk that same balance beam when seeking to inspire, without overwhelming the listener with potential risks, which can create a paralyzing fear.

Camelot Meets Castro

President Kennedy had to walk this realism tightrope more than once when dealing with Russia's Khrushchev and Cuba's Castro. He had already been burned by his attempts during the Bay of Pigs fiasco to oust the lead man in Cuba, and tensions with the Communist nations were high. In the fall of his second year in office, President Kennedy faced a crisis that could send the United States spiraling quickly from the Cold War into a cold sweat. Soviet leader, Khrushchev, had secretly sent long-range nuclear missiles and other atomic weapons to Cuba, along with tens of thousands of Soviet troops.

After days of classified meetings and private consultation with his national security team, the president opted to respond first with a naval blockade before bringing the crisis to the attention of the American public. While he eventually did speak publicly of a possible nuclear strike due to the buildup of weaponry in Cuba by the Soviet Union, he only did so after he had a plan and negotiating tools in place to thwart the threat. Many believe that Kennedy was able to strategize around full-scale public panic, by first curbing the crisis with his personal discipline and then informing the public in a position of negotiating strength, rather than a barrage alarming facts. As a result of Kennedy's careful approach to crisis, the country was inspired to defend and protect, rather than cower and hide.

After a series of personal difficulties, Harvard Business School historian Nancy Koehn studied five leaders and how they handled themselves in a crisis. In her book *Forged in a Crisis: The Power of Courageous Leadership in Turbulent Times,* she examines several stages of crisis leadership. She coined the phrase "gathering periods" for one of those stages. Like Kennedy, this is the time leaders spend first filling themselves with strength and purpose, and then training themselves to be slow to react in a crisis. According to Koehn, this important gathering period of strength and wisdom can play out for years. She dissects what has happened during these times and how it eventually manifests itself when leadership requires a response:

> *What's happening to these people during these [gathering] moments? They are investing in themselves. They're learning a great deal about their thinking and possible contribution to the great events of the day. Those periods of not accomplishing things externally were, instead, about building their equipment inside—emotionally, intellectually, and in some cases spiritually—to be ready for their moment. They're not losing sight of the big picture and the stage on which they're going to make a big difference. These are people who commit to getting better*

from the inside out. These gathering years are important for our millennial students to understand. Your moment doesn't always have to happen in a dramatic, made-for-the-movies way when you're twenty-seven. You prepare yourself for the next big move you'll make, but you can't make that move until you understand the stage.[72]

As Obama mentioned in his health care speech, approaching the health care crisis isn't a rah-rah moment. Neither are gathering periods. Obama knew from his years of legislative experience that he must patiently educate the public and then endure public opinion in order to even approach a solution to the crisis. Kennedy, also, drew upon his years in public office, and his own trials with Cuba, to eventually inspire the country to avoid reaction during the Cold War. Inspiration is often the result of leaders who employ their years of "gathering moments," to shape their understanding of the facts and details of a crisis. Only then, with a large dose of realism and positivity, should they select their words, actions, and motives to inspire a collective, productive response.

America will never know—and has never needed to know—just how close we came to a nuclear event with Cuba. But we were inspired to protect ourselves, and one another, under a leader who chose just what to say, and what to leave out.

LEADERS INSPIRE BY EMPOWERING OTHERS

When John F. Kennedy was first elected president, many felt that a youthful, invigorating post-war idealism had quickly settled in the White House. As the historian Arthur M. Schlesinger Jr., Kennedy's friend and adviser, later wrote, "The capital city, somnolent in the Eisenhower years, had suddenly come alive ... [with] the release of energy which occurs when men with ideas have a chance to put them into practice."[73]

No program illustrates that youthful idealism better than the creation of the Peace Corps, which was established by executive order at the beginning of Kennedy's administration. A volunteer program designed to impact social and economic development abroad, President Kennedy's creation has since invigorated and empowered almost a quarter million volunteers—mostly young, single Americans—who have served in over 140 countries. President Kennedy harnessed the growing excitement of postwar development and used his new program to empower the leaders of tomorrow to believe that they can make a difference.

Yes We Can!

On March 30, 2016, President Obama stopped by the famous 14th Street Washington D.C. eatery, Busboys and Poets, to visit with former inmates who had been recently released under his Clemency Project initiative. At the time, the president was well on his way to becoming the first commander in chief to substantively address the social, moral, political, and economic epidemic created by mass incarceration. Through an initiative called Clemency Project 2014, the president offered nonviolent federal inmates the opportunity to apply for relief through the Department of Justice's Office of the Pardon Attorney. Working cooperatively with other programs, such as Families Against Mandatory Minimums, President Obama was not only focused on the relief granted to those who received commutation, but also their chances at successful reentry into society. This special luncheon was hosted on a day that the president had granted an additional sixty-one commutations to former inmates suffering under harsh sentences for drug charges.

During lunch, the president pointed out the inmates who had successfully reintegrated and become productive citizens of society. He sought to build not only the confidence in his criminal justice reform efforts, but also in the individuals who were facing the challenges of living life in the free world. His initiatives were meant to bring relief and build confidence in those who had previously been forgotten, neglected, or left without much hope. President Obama called that luncheon an opportunity to "show people what second chances look like."[74]

Leadership provides one of the greatest opportunities to build confidence and competency in others.

Often, it includes the rare opportunity to offer someone a much-needed second chance. There is enormous power in the three simple words, "Yes we can!" It put the first black president in office, it informed inmates that they could thrive in a world without bars, it has inspired humans to walk on the moon, and it continues to inspire individuals to change the world.

No matter your political persuasion, as a leader causing others to believe, "Yes we can" is a powerful tool. Leaders must often remind their followers of the opportunities and the belief those dreams can be achieved. We tend to give up on ourselves before others give up on us, and leaders are believers in the abilities of those who often do not yet see it. As a child, I was told by the then current head football coach of the Miami Hurricanes that "to believe is to be strong." Not everyone believes in themselves, and leaders have a great opportunity to bring strength and vision to others.

Be the Leader Your Dog Thinks You Are

Sometimes I wish I believed in myself as much as my dog believes in me. Lincoln, our family Goldendoodle, looks at me like I just solved world hunger. When I literally throw him a bone, he celebrates the bone—and me—with great joy and exuberance. I can't read his mind, but I'm sure he's thinking I'm the greatest human on the planet. I often remind myself to be the kind of person my dog thinks I am.

Similarly, I tell my kids to believe in themselves. I look at them with the same love and affection that my dog looks at me. I remember telling my oldest daughter who was struggling with a career pathway and a big interview to believe in herself. I told her, "You believed in Santa for eight years. Surely you can believe in yourself today." Sometimes we need fans in our corner looking at us with those eyes and telling us to believe in ourselves.

In his 2008 presidential acceptance speech, President-elect Obama highlighted the story of 106-year-old Ann Nixon Cooper as an example of the great perseverance and character that lives in all of us. Obama chose her as his embodiment of "Yes *you* can" to inspire the nation into new hope.

> At a time when women's voices were silenced and their hopes dismissed, she lived to see them stand up and speak out and reach for the ballot. Yes we can.
>
> When there was despair in the Dust Bowl and Depression across the land, she saw a nation conquer fear itself with a New Deal, new jobs, a new sense of common purpose. Yes we can.
>
> When the bombs fell on our harbor and tyranny threatened the world, she was there to witness a generation rise to greatness and a democracy was saved. Yes we can.
>
> She was there for the buses in Montgomery, the hoses in Birmingham, a bridge in Selma, and a preacher from Atlanta who told a people that "We Shall Overcome." Yes we can.
>
> A man touched down on the moon, a wall came down in Berlin, a world was connected by our own science and imagination. And this year, in this election, she touched her finger to a screen, and cast her vote, because after 106 years in America, through the best

of times and the darkest of hours, she knows how America can change. Yes we can.

America, we have come so far. We have seen so much. But there is so much more to do. So tonight, let us ask ourselves—if our children should live to see the next century, if my daughters should be so lucky to live as long as Ann Nixon Cooper, what change will they see? What progress will we have made? This is our chance to answer that call. This is our moment.[75]

As leaders, you are the one—like President Obama—who gets to make this call. You are the one whose voice can inspire others to first believe great things in themselves so they can do great things. You are the one who can be the leader your dog thinks you are, so that you can tell others what they need to believe about themselves.

Guess Who's Coming to Dinner

When Ray Kinsella sat and surveyed his handiwork hewn out of a cornfield, he was amazed by all the baseball greats who appeared on his Field of Dreams. He respected that there were so many who had preceded him in the game and had stepped up to the plate to shape the sport he loved.

President Obama and President Kennedy were both hosts at a table that had been set by many greats who had gone before them. They were able to serve the meal of equality and inspiration, thanks to a long depth chart of players whose home runs and sacrifices provided the sustenance they needed to feed a nation in need of hope. Kennedy served up the dream. Obama shared a meal of "Yes we can!" And they both respected the others who previously played on their team.

Both #35 and #44 dreamed, and then they did something about it. President Kennedy sent youth out into the world, believing they could do great things. President Obama gathered them back in to remind them of the great things they have done.

Be the leader who gathers and sends. Dream the impossible and inspire action. Keep it real and keep it positive. Go the distance and heal some pain. And heed President Obama's call, "Change will not come if we wait for some other person or if we wait for some other time. We are the ones we've been waiting for."

FINAL THOUGHTS ON LEADERSHIP With

Jimmy Carter & John Quincy Adams

Leaders Never Stop

"My faith demands that I do whatever I can, wherever I am,
whenever I can, for as long as I can, with whatever I have
to try and make a difference."
–Jimmy Carter

"Leadership is not about the next election,
it's about the next generation."
–Simon Sinek

I n the early 2000s, I had the privilege of speaking with my father at an event. My father is one of my greatest role models for leadership. Sharing the stage with him was an honor—and a moment of pride as a son. The highlight of the event, however, was not just the opportunity for us to speak together, but the encounter with a man we met afterwards.

An older gentleman in the crowd approached us after the conference to share a bit of his life story. While striking in stature, he carried himself in an ordinary manner. He was your "run of the mill" senior adult man with a gentle voice and large frame. As he opened up about his career, I was amazed to discover that he had spent the better part of his scientific career working on product development for a new drug called ibuprofen. Although he wasn't the inventor of the drug, he was responsible for marketing and developing the drug for mass distribution. I'm not sure what I thought the people behind ibuprofen looked like, but he wasn't who I expected. He continued to describe the process of development, test trials, and his constant prayers that he didn't harm anyone in the testing process. After describing his storied career in great detail, we asked what he was doing now. His reply startled me. "I try to volunteer at my church, but all they ask me to do is put pencils in the pews for church each Sunday."

Don't get me wrong. When you are serving in the church, there are no jobs that are too small. But I just had to wonder what had happened. Before me was a man who spent his career developing a universal drug, seemingly reduced to spending his talents putting pencils in pew racks at his church. As the man walked away from us that day, I couldn't help but ponder that this was probably not how he envisioned spending the final years of his life.

There's a lot to be said for finishing strong. That part of the journey depends largely on the individual, but I believe everyone wants to breathe their last breath knowing they were valuable participants until the end. Many want to be difference makers, not just in their lifetime, but also leave an impact beyond the span of their years.

In order to finish strong as a lifetime difference maker, you have to embrace the concept that leaders never stop.

I don't believe anyone is best served by concluding a lifetime of great leadership by stuffing pencils into the pew of life. So, as I draw this book to a close, let me briefly share with you two ways leaders never stop and call upon two more presidents to serve as role models.

LEADERS NEVER STOP SERVING

John Quincy Adams spent seventeen years of his post presidential life serving in the United States House of Representatives. A passionate abolitionist, Adams fought hard to abolish the slave trade and restore dignity to the men and women of color. Like his father, President John Adams—who defended the British soldiers following the Boston Massacre—John Quincy was willing to take on unpopular cases in order to fight for justice.

In 1839, a Spanish slave ship, *La Amistad,* was overtaken by the captive Africans enslaved on the vessel and the crew was held hostage. Threatened with their lives, the sailors agreed to return the Africans back to their native homeland. However, the crew instead made way for New York where the ship was taken into custody by the U.S. Navy.

After a series of court trials, Adams somewhat reluctantly agreed to take the case as his last great work of service to the nation. Nicknamed *Old Man Eloquent,* Adams argued on behalf of the slaves and ultimately won before the Supreme Court. Over a decade after leaving the Executive Mansion (as the White House was known back then), Adams was still serving his nation and pursuing the good of all mankind.

Leaders never stop serving. As simple as that statement sounds, it's actually rather difficult. My father and I have regular conversations about the struggle many leaders feel in retirement. They climb the mountain of their careers, receive a gold watch as a gift, then feel shoved down the other side of the mountain into the oblivion of retirement. Many great leaders who have taken that plunge believe they will never be an influencer or leader again. They buy into the lie that without an official position, they are no longer in a place of leadership. Nothing could be further from the truth. While the *position* of leadership may change over time—and one day there may be no authoritative leadership position that fits on a resume—the *posture* of leadership never stops. In other words, bloom where you're planted—even if that is not in an official position.

True leaders are constantly seeking opportunities to lead the next generation. Though the legitimacy of this quote being attributed to John Quincy Adams is debated, he is quoted by many as saying, "If your actions inspire others to dream more, learn more, do more, and become more, you are a leader." These words speak truth, irrespective of who originally spoke them. You will notice that nothing in that quote indicates job title, office location, or an age younger than sixty-five. It speaks merely of the actions that indicate leadership—at any age, in any location, with or without a title. If this book has communicated any truth, I hope it has reminded you that no matter where life finds you today, you are a leader.

LEADERS NEVER STOP INFLUENCING

> *"My mother's influence was to take on new challenges and do what I thought was right even though sometimes the consequences politically speaking were not good. My mother was vivacious, she was full of life, she got up every morning looking forward to the day, trying to figure out what she could do that was innovative and unprecedented and maybe controversial."*[76]
> –Jimmy Carter

Most agree that there has been no post presidential life more productive and prolific than Jimmy Carter's. In fact, more people associate Carter with his work after office than while serving in the presidency. He certainly serves as an example of a leader who never stops.

Jimmy Carter's name has become synonymous with the organization Habitat for Humanity. This worthy effort has been in existence since 1942 and is credited with building houses around the world for more than twenty-nine million people. In fact, some of the proceeds from this book help support Habitat's work of bringing strength and stability to people's lives by providing places of shelter. While many of the people associated with Habitat may not be household names, Jimmy and Rosalyn Carter certainly are their most famous volunteers. According to Habitat for Humanity, "President and Mrs. Carter have worked alongside 103,000 volunteers in fourteen countries to build, renovate, and repair 4,331 homes."[77] This does not measure the influence the Carters have had upon countless volunteers around the world. Though no longer in office, Jimmy Carter has demonstrated his ongoing commitment to use his influence for good.

Irrespective of age and title, leaders are always influencers. An interesting phenomenon of human nature takes place as we grow older. As teenagers, we assume no one is looking to us as leaders and we believe we don't really have a voice in people's lives. As we climb the ladder of our careers and people are placed under our leadership, we start believing we have a voice and maybe even something to share. As we age into retirement, we again embrace those lies of our youth that no one is interested in what we have to offer and the leadership insights we have to contribute. If you find yourself in such a place, I want to invite you to stop believing your own lies.

You have probably told a teenager at one point of your life that they are influencers. In fact, for this generation, "influencer" has become an actual job title. I recently attended a retreat of young adults and nearly half the people in the group referred to themselves as "influencers." You may need to assume that new millennial title for yourself. If you'll look around you, you'll find many people who could use some direction, a mentor, or just a word of encouragement. There are young leaders who are starving for someone farther down the road of life to invest in them. You have life experiences and lessons from the school of hard knocks that can make a real difference in the lives of people. But you will only continue to be effective if you quit believing the lie that says no one views you as a leader anymore. If your leadership is based only on a position, you're not really a leader—you've merely managed a role. True leaders never stop influencing people.

Take the time to ask yourself, who is that person in your life that might benefit from a little time with you? Is there someone you need to invite to coffee? Is there someone behind you in the leadership pipeline who could benefit from your years of wisdom? The key to this line of thinking is that you can't stop or view it as a temporary shift.

I'm a fan of relaxation, but too many people are wasting their influence on a hobby to keep them busy. With a little effort, they could be helping to construct a foundation for future leaders and providing the wisdom of experience. If Jimmy Carter has the time to give of himself in big and small ways, you probably do as well.

A New Day Coming

On February 23, 1848, John Quincy Adams died suddenly of a stroke. He literally died doing what he loved—serving in the United States Congress. After voting to table a motion, he collapsed at his desk. Adams was taken to the Speaker's office where he lingered for two days and then passed away quietly. Some believed him to murmur, "This is the last of earth. I am composed."

A committee was formed to plan the funeral of our sixth president. One member of that committee was a young congressman from Illinois named Abraham Lincoln. A new generation was burying the old and preparing for the new.

There is always a new day coming. New leaders will emerge as others fade from the scene. But be careful not to fade before your time. That new, upcoming generation wants to hear from you and needs to understand you. Your children may have not listened to you growing up, but your grandchildren are hungry to hear the lessons of life you have to share. Keep speaking into the next generation. Look for opportunities to impart wisdom whether it's through a conversation over coffee, an email sent, or a book you write. But never stop serving. Never stop leading. Never stop acting upon the influence you have built throughout your life.

John Wesley, the great itinerant preacher and founder of the Methodist church, once said, "Do all the good you can. By all the means you can. In all the ways you can. In all the places you can. At all the times you can. To all the people you can. As long as ever you can."

Leaders are inherently action figures. Whether you find yourself at the beginning of your career, at the end, or somewhere in between, the calling upon your life to lead others has never been a product of power or position. It is based on the truth that you are here for a reason—to make a difference in this world.

The Presidents of the United States were imperfect people who felt the call to lead the nation. Your opportunity to lead may not seem as significant as theirs, but your responsibility is just as grand. Don't sit on the sidelines or let your deficiencies define you. Engage whatever opportunity is available and lead others into a better tomorrow.

Like the presidents, solemnly swear to execute your role as a leader to the best of your ability. And then, never stop.

Acknowledgments

The presidency ultimately is not about one individual, but about an administration. No single individual can govern a great nation like ours alone. I am certain the same could be said about getting a book from an idea all the way to print. This book has been a partnership among many friends who have walked alongside me to the finish line. I want to mention some below with apologies to the many I am inadvertently leaving out.

I am deeply indebted to two women who poured their hearts into this book. First, I am grateful to Mindi Bach. I will always remember that first conversation where I shared with you all I had written so far and by the end of our discussion, we had completely rewritten the book. Thank you for pushing me to think more deeply, write more directly, and believe this project could be bigger than I had originally imagined. And thank you to Jana Good, our detailed editor who made this book better through meticulous questions, pushback on sections she deemed superfluous, and affirmation that drove us forward. Both of you are treasures to me and without these two women, this project would probably still be incomplete.

I am also grateful for the historians and leaders who allowed me to interview them for this project. I am grateful to have spent time talking to one of our greatest living historians, Richard Brookhiser, to discuss the life of James Madison. Holly Kuzmich, (executive director of the George W. Bush Institute and senior vice president of the George W. Bush Presidential Center) lent her insights into President George W. Bush and his process of making decisions. My conversation with Jim McGrath (vice president of the George H.W. Bush Foundation) was so helpful as we sat in the private office used by President George H.W. Bush and discussed the president's incredible relationship-building expertise. Thank you also to Stephanie Streett (executive director at the Clinton Foundation) and Bruce Lindsay (board of directors, Clinton Foundation) for our time together at the Bill Clinton Presidential Library discussing the "New Covenant" and a place called Hope. Finally, thank you to Mark Updegrove, president and CEO of the LBJ Foundation, who not only allowed me to sit at LBJ's private dining table to discuss the "Johnson Treatment" but also graciously agreed to write the foreword to this book.

I must also express my appreciation to the many docents, tour guides, and park rangers at the presidential libraries, homes, and museums I toured as part of the research for this book. I may not know your names, but I am grateful for how you teach history to thousands of visitors each year. It is people like these who keep history alive.

I also want to express my thanks to my publisher, Morgan James Publishing, and to the CEO, David Hancock. David not only believed in the project from the start but even contributed his expertise on President Ronald Reagan. Thank you to Margo Toulouse for helping to shepherd this project through to the finish line. There are many others at Morgan James who are behind the scenes but were instrumental in making this book a reality. Thank you.

The teeth of my leadership were cut at the wonderful church I get the privilege of pastoring—First Baptist Church at The Fields. Thank you to my friends and staff who have become my extended family over these more than two decades of working together. Of all people, when you read this book, you know there are some of these principles I may apply well and others that are still works in progress in me as a leader. Thank you for believing in me as a young leader, and still believing in me as the word "young" no longer fits.

To my extended family that is Presidential Leadership Scholars, I say thank you. I never dreamed when we first met in 2016 of the influence so many of you would have on my life. I dedicated this book to you because you have all made me a better leader as we studied modern leadership through the lens of four presidents. We don't agree on everything (except the bacon at the Clinton Library), but we all deeply want the best for our nation. I'm proud to know you and call you my friends.

Finally, I could not do anything I do without the loving support of my family. I will always be grateful to my parents for instilling in me a love of history and leadership. My wife, Allison, and our three children are constant encouragers to me and have patiently endured when we needed to alter plans to stop by a particular historical site. Thank you for your love and grace to me, especially when I had to work on the book. Family is everything.

Theodore Roosevelt once said, "If you could kick the person in the pants responsible for most of your trouble, you wouldn't sit for a month." In other words, any errors you find in this book all belong to me.

When I was five years old, my maternal grandparents gave me a record (you young people can google it). It was called *Young Abe Lincoln*. I used to lie on the floor and listen to the songs about Captain Lincoln fighting in the Black Hawk War. To this day, I chart my love for presidents, and specifically Abraham Lincoln, back to that small gift.

I am reminded that you never know the influence you might have on future generations. My grandparents gave me a gift that sparked a love for history and presidents. You have a gift as well. How you share that gift with others could make an incredible difference in someone's life for years to come. That is the essence of leadership—sharing your gifts and talents to change the world.

Resources

Presidential Libraries

This book would not have been possible without the existence and inspiration of the Presidential Libraries and Museums and those who lead them. These national treasures, for many, are unknown resources for each presidential administrations and the history surrounding that era.

I want to invite you to consider visiting our Presidential Libraries and Museums, or at least seeking the resources they have available online. The National Archives and Records Administration oversees the Presidential Libraries dating back to Herbert Hoover, and has managed a technologically advanced system to bring that material to the public. Many other presidents than are mentioned in this book have museums and libraries that I also encourage you to visit. Take your family and spend a day learning about these great leaders who guided our nation and interacting with life in the Oval Office and beyond.

Libraries operated by the National Archives and Records Administration:

Herbert Hoover Library and Museum
210 Parkside Drive
West Branch, IA 52358-0488
hoover.library@nara.gov

Franklin D. Roosevelt Presidential Library and Museum
4079 Albany Post Road
Hyde Park, NY 12538-1999
https://fdrlibrary.org

Harry S. Truman Presidential Library and Museum
500 West U.S. Highway 24
Independence, MO 64050-1798
http://www.trumanlibrary.gov

Dwight D. Eisenhower Presidential Library and Museum
200 SE 4th Street
Abilene, KS 67410-2900
https://eisenhowerlibrary.gov

John F. Kennedy Presidential Library and Museum
Columbia Point
Boston, MA 02125-3398
http://www.jfklibrary.org

Lyndon B. Johnson Presidential Library and Museum
2313 Red River Street
Austin, TX 78705-5702
http://www.lbjlibrary.org

Richard M. Nixon Library
18001 Yorba Linda Blvd.
Yorba Linda, CA 92886
nixon@nara.gov

Gerald R. Ford Museum
303 Pearl Street, NW
Grand Rapids, MI 49504-5353
http://www.fordlibrarymuseum.gov

Jimmy Carter Presidential Library and Museum
441 Freedom Parkway
Atlanta, GA 30307-1498
http://www.jimmycarterlibrary.gov

Ronald Reagan Presidential Library and Museum
40 Presidential Drive
Simi Valley, CA 93065-0600
http://www.reaganlibrary.gov

George Bush Presidential Library and Museum
1000 George Bush Drive West
College Station, TX 77845
https://bush41library.tamu.edu

William J. Clinton Presidential Library and Museum
1200 President Clinton Avenue
Little Rock, Arkansas 72201
https://www.clintonlibrary.gov

George W. Bush Presidential Library and Museum
2943 SMU Boulevard
Dallas, TX 75205
http://www.georgewbushlibrary.smu.edu

About the Author

B rent Taylor, D. Min., is a pastor, international speaker, professor of American history, and corporate communicator. He is the author of *Founding Leadership: Lessons on Business and Personal Leadership from the Men Who Brought You the American Revolution*. Brent enjoys reading great stories from history, fishing, traveling, and helping people find their purpose in life. His other great passion is discovering the red light on at Krispy Kreme Donuts. Brent lives in the Dallas, Texas, area with his wife, three children, and dog, Lincoln. For more information or to contact Brent about a speaking engagement, go to DrBrentTaylor.com.

Mindi Bach is a freelance writer, speaker, financial advisor and educator. She has written and contributed to books and articles on a variety of topics—recently coauthoring a book with a former NFL player and federal inmate. Mindi enjoys sports, the outdoors, and penning theological, coffee-fueled limericks. She holds a B.A. in Political Science from UCLA and resides in Boise, Idaho, with her family.

Endnotes

1 "George Washington: The Reluctant President." *Smithsonian.com*, Smithsonian Institution, 1 Feb. 2011, www.smithsonianmag.com/ history/george-washington-the-reluctant-president-49492/.

2 Janaraghi, Parissa. "Ford v Ferrari Best Movie Quotes 'We're Going to Make History'." *Movie Quotes and More*, 14 Jan. 2020, www. moviequotesandmore.com/ford-v-ferrari-best-movie-quotes/.

3 "Clinton's Covenant: New Choice Based on Old Values." *The Independent*, Independent Digital News and Media, 18 Sept. 2011, www.independent.co.uk/news/clintons-covenant-new-choice-based-on-old-values-5598121.html.

4 Clinton. "Thank Bill Clinton for AmeriCorps." *Medium*, The Clinton Foundation, 9 Aug. 2017, stories.clintonfoundation.org/thank-bill-clinton-for-americorps-30c1de468365.

5 About the author(s) This interview was conducted by Hans-Werner Kaas. "Bill Ford Charts a Course for the Future." *McKinsey & Company*, www.mckinsey.com/industries/automotive-and-assembly/ our-insights/bill-ford-charts-a-course-for-the-future.

6   About the author(s) This interview was conducted by Hans-Werner Kaas. "Bill Ford Charts a Course for the Future." *McKinsey & Company*, www.mckinsey.com/industries/automotive-and-assembly/ our-insights/bill-ford-charts-a-course-for-the-future.

7   "How a 'Dream Big' Global Health Partnership Is Saving the Lives of Millions." *An Oral History of PEPFAR: How a "Dream Big" Partnership Is Saving the Lives of Millions*, www.bushcenter.org/publications/ essays/pepfar.html.

8   McCullough, David. *Truman*. Simon & Schuster, 1992, pp 734

9   Arguello, Lorenzo. "16 Awesome Anecdotes About the Dream Team And Its Megastar Players." *Business Insider*, Business Insider, 16 July 2012, www.businessinsider.com/the-dream-team-2012-7.

10 McCullough, David. *Truman*. Simon & Schuster, 1992, pp 559-560

11 Presidential Podcast - Truman

12 McCullough, David. *Truman*. Simon & Schuster, 1992, pp 443-444

13 McCullough, David. *Truman*. Simon & Schuster, 1992, pp 546-547

14 *EX-99.1*, www.sec.gov/Archives/edgar/ data/1018724/000119312517120198/d373368dex991.htm.

15 "Interviews - Wayne Slater | The Choice 2004 | FRONTLINE." *PBS*, Public Broadcasting Service, 12 Oct. 2004, www.pbs.org/ wgbh/pages/frontline/shows/choice2004/interviews/slater.html.

16 "Financial Crisis." *Decision Points*, by George W. Bush, Crown Publ., 2010, pp. 439–472.

17 Masters of scale. "Eric Schmidt on Masters of Scale with Reid Hoffman." *Wait What*, Wait What, 10 Dec. 2019, mastersofscale. com/eric-schmidt-innovation-managed-chaos/.

18 Jones, Yolanda. "Alice Johnson Granted Clemency, Returns to Memphis: 'I Am so Grateful'." *The Commercial Appeal*, The Commercial Appeal, 7 June 2018, www.commercialappeal.com/story/ news/2018/06/07/alive-marie-johnson-savors-freedom-back-home-memphis/680631002/.

19   Doug. "Text - H.R.5682 - 115th Congress (2017-2018): FIRST
     STEP Act." *Congress.gov*, 23 May 2018, www.congress.gov/
     bill/115th-congress/house-bill/5682/text.

20   "Jones: Give Trump Credit on Prison Reform - CNN Video." *CNN*,
     Cable News Network, 15 Nov. 2018, www.cnn.com/videos/politics/
     2018/11/15/van-jones-trump-criminal-justice-reform-credit-ctn-vpx.cnn.

21   Iger, Robert. "'We Could Say Anything to Each Other': Bob Iger
     Remembers Steve Jobs." *Vanity Fair*, Vanity Fair, 18 Sept. 2019,
     www.vanityfair.com/news/2019/09/bob-iger-remembers-steve-jobs.

22   Rupert Cornwell Washington @IndyVoices. "Muhammad Ali Was a
     One-off Who Came to Define an Era." *The Independent*, Independent
     Digital News and Media, 5 June 2016, www.independent.co.uk/
     news/people/muhammad-ali-dead-appreciation-came-to-define-an-
     era-a7065161.html.

23   https://twitter.com/realDonaldTrump/status/1199718185865535490/
     photo/1?ref_src=twsrc%5Etfw%7Ctwcamp%5Etweetembed%7C
     twterm%5E1199718185865535490&ref_url=https%3A%2F%2F
     deadline.com%2F2019%2F11%2Fdonald-trump-rocky-tweet-
     sylvester-stallone-1202796475%2F

24   Kaczynski, Andrew. "Whitaker Said He Supports State's Rights to
     Nullify Federal Law." *CNN*, Cable News Network, 10 Nov. 2018,
     www.cnn.com/2018/11/09/politics/matthew-whitaker-nullification/
     index.html.

25   Hamilton, Bethany, et al. *Soul Surfer: A True Story of Faith, Family,
     and Fighting to Get Back on the Board*. Pocket Books, 2012.

26   *Bill Clinton, Time Magazine, June 24, 2009 "Getting It Right"*

27   "Strategic Alliances - Types and Benefits of Strategic Alliances."
     Corporate Finance Institute, corporatefinanceinstitute.com/
     resources/knowledge/strategy/strategic-alliances/.

28   *https://medium.com/the-gentle-revolution/social-courage-8ef4b3ca8404*

29 "The Culmination." *Roosevelt: The Lion and the Fox*, by James M. Burns, Harcourt Brace Jovanovich, 1956, p. 477.

30 History.com Editors. "Franklin D. Roosevelt." *History.com*, A&E Television Networks, 29 Oct. 2009, www.history.com/topics/us-presidents/franklin-d-roosevelt.

31 https://www.psychologytoday.com/blog/the-squeaky-wheel/201508/seven-ways-boost-your-emotional-courage

32 Wagner, James. "Mark DeRosa Read Theodore Roosevelt Speech to Nationals before Game 4." *The Washington Post*, WP Company, 11 Oct. 2012, www.washingtonpost.com/news/nationals-journal/wp/2012/10/11/mark-derosa-read-theodore-roosevelt-speech-to-nationals-before-game-4/?arc404=true.

33 "'More Important Than Gold': FDR's First Fireside Chat." *HISTORY MATTERS: The U.S. Survey Course on the Web*, historymatters.gmu.edu/d/5199/.

34 Montanaro, Domenico. "George H.W. Bush's Life has Plenty of Lessons for Today's Politics." *NPR*, NPR, 3 Dec. 2018, www.npr.org/2018/12/03/672696198/george-h-w-bushs-life-has-plenty-of-lessons-for-today-s-politics.

35 *Grant*, by Ron Chernow, Penguin Books, 2018, pp. 638–640.

36 Shafer, Ronald G. "The President Who Fired a Special Prosecutor in 1875." *The Washington Post*, WP Company, 18 Dec. 2018, www.washingtonpost.com/history/2018/12/18/crosshairs-an-investigation-president-fired-special-prosecutor/.

37 Farrell, John A., et al. "The Year Nixon Fell Apart." *POLITICO Magazine*, 26 Mar. 2017, www.politico.com/magazine/story/2017/03/john-farrell-nixon-book-excerpt-214954.

38 Neagle, David. "What Being Embezzled Out of $5 Million Taught Me About Forgiveness and Moving On." *Entrepreneur*, 7 Dec. 2018, www.entrepreneur.com/article/323585.

39 John. "Warren Buffett Looks for These 3 Traits in People When He Hires Them." *Business Insider*, Business Insider, 4 Jan. 2017, www.businessinsider.com/what-warren-buffett-looks-for-in-candidates-2017-1.

40 "Ghost Rider (Robbie Reyes)." *Ultimate Marvel Cinematic Universe Wikia*, ultimate-marvel-cinematic-universe.fandom.com/wiki/Ghost_Rider_(Robbie_Reyes).

41 Zelizer, Julian E. "The New Enemies List." *The Atlantic*, Atlantic Media Company, 4 Sept. 2018, www.theatlantic.com/ideas/archive/2018/08/the-new-enemies-list/567874/.

42 "Home." *Water gate info*, watergate.info/impeachment/articles-of-impeachment.

43 Burlingame, Michael, and Connecticut College. "Abraham Lincoln: Impact and Legacy." *Miller Center*, 23 July 2018, millercenter.org/president/lincoln/impact-and-legacy.

44 *The History Place: Abraham Lincoln: Message to Ulysses S. Grant*, www.historyplace.com/lincoln/lett-5.htm.

45 https://www.nytimes.com/2014/05/04/books/review/james-madison-by-lynne-cheney.html

46 https://medium.com/@ameet/5-leadership-lessons-from-bob-iger-ceo-of-disney-92512b7efc1f

47 Interview, Mark Updegrove, LBJ Library, Houston, Texas

48 Saturday Morning Tea, Tony Bridwell, B2B Books, 2020.

49 "James Madison." *James Madison*, by Richard Brookhiser, Basic Books, 2013, p. 74.

50 https://www.salesforce.com/blog/2017/07/impact-of-equality-business-research.html?d=7010M000001yv8PQAQ)

51 Gallo, Carmine. "Steve Jobs: The World's Greatest Business Storyteller." *The World's Greatest Business Storyteller*, 8 Oct. 2015, www.forbes.com/sites/carminegallo/2015/10/08/steve-jobs-the-worlds-greatest-business-storyteller.

52 *Saturday Morning Tea*, Tony Bridwell

53 https://history.howstuffworks.com/historical-figures/ridiculous-history-lbj-talked-the-phone-more-a-teenager.htm

54 "Mr. President." *James Madison: A Life Reconsidered*, by Lynne V. Cheney, Penguin Books, 2015, pp. 353–354.

55 *The History Place: Great Speeches Collection: Ronald Reagan Speech 'Tear Down This Wall'*, www.historyplace.com/speeches/reagan-tear-down.htm.

56 Edwards, Gavin. "We Are the World: A Minute-by-Minute Breakdown." *Rolling Stone*, 25 June 2018, www.rollingstone.com/music/music-features/we-are-the-world-a-minute-by-minute-breakdown-54619/.

57 Cannon, Lou. "Ronald Reagan: Foreign Affairs." *Miller Center*, 11 July 2017, millercenter.org/president/reagan/foreign-affairs.

58 "Ronald Reagan." *The Independent*, Independent Digital News and Media, 20 Sept. 2012, www.independent.co.uk/news/presidents/ronald-reagan-1482923.html.

59 "Bold Action Is Needed for GM to Achieve Mary Barra's Stretching Vision." *Clean Technica*, 7 Sept. 2018, cleantechnica.com/2018/09/06/bold-action-is-needed-for-gm-to-achieve-mary-barras-stretching-vision/.

60 LaReau, Jamie L. "General Motors Reveals Its Vision of the Future for the UAW Workforce." *Detroit Free Press*, Detroit Free Press, 30 Oct. 2019, www.freep.com/story/money/cars/general-motors/2019/10/30/gm-future-cars-uaw-workforce/2496303001/.

61 "U.S. Air Force Doctrine > Home." *U.S. Air Force Doctrine > Home*, www.doctrine.af.mil/.

62 "Authentic Leadership: Enabling Individuals John Maxwell Company." *John Maxwell Company*, 9 July 2019, corporatesolutions.johnmaxwell.com/blog/authentic-leadership-enabling-individuals/.

63 Ambar, Saladin, and Rutgers University-New Brunswick. "Woodrow Wilson: Impact and Legacy." *Miller Center*, 30 Aug. 2017, millercenter.org/president/wilson/impact-and-legacy.

64 "Civil Rights Movement." *JFK Library*, www.jfklibrary.org/learn/about-jfk/jfk-in-history/civil-rights-movement

65 "Change Comes to America." *The Presidential Campaign of Barack Obama a Critical Analysis of a Racially Transcendent Strategy*, by Dewey M. Clayton, Routledge, 2010, pp. 160–161.

66 "Field of Dreams." *IMDb*, IMDb.com, www.imdb.com/title/tt0097351/characters/nm0000469.

67 "Chicago." *Dreams from My Father: a Story of Race and Inheritance*, by Barack OBAMA, Canongate, 2007, p. 190.

68 Levingston, Steven. "John F. Kennedy, Martin Luther King Call Changed History." *Time*, Time, 20 June 2017, time.com/4817240/martin-luther-king-john-kennedy-phone-call/.

69 "Shoe Dog." *Shoe Dog*, by Phil Knight, Simon & Schuster, 2018, p. 382.

70 "JFK RICE MOON SPEECH." *NASA*, NASA, er.jsc.nasa.gov/seh/ricetalk.htm.

71 "Remarks by the President on the Affordable Care Act." *National Archives and Records Administration*, National Archives and Records Administration, obamawhitehouse.archives.gov/the-press-office/2016/10/20/remarks-president-affordable-care-act.

72 "Five Leaders Forged in Crisis, and What We Can Learn from Them." *HBS Working Knowledge*, 4 Oct. 2017, hbswk.hbs.edu/item/5-leaders-forged-in-crisis-and-what-we-can-learn-from-them.

73 Brinkley, Alan. "The Legacy of John F. Kennedy." *The Atlantic*, Atlantic Media Company, 19 Feb. 2014, www.theatlantic.com/magazine/archive/2013/08/the-legacy-of-john-f-kennedy/309499/.

74 Fabian, Jordan. "Obama Takes Former Prisoners out to Lunch." *The Hill*, 30 Mar. 2016, thehill.com/blogs/ballot-box/presidential-races/274691-obama-takes-former-prisoners-out-to-lunch.

75 "Transcript of Barack Obama's Victory Speech." *NPR*, NPR, 5 Nov. 2008, www.npr.org/templates/story/story.php?storyId=96624326.

76 Toby Harnden, US Editor. "Transcript of the Interview with Former US President Jimmy Carter." *The Telegraph*, Telegraph Media Group, 29 Apr. 2008, www.telegraph.co.uk/news/politics/local-elections/1908059/Transcript-of-the-interview-with-former-US-President-Jimmy-Carter.html.

77 "Carter Work Project." *Habitat for Humanity*, 11 Oct. 2019, www.habitat.org/volunteer/build-events/carter-work-project.